Networks of Champions

Networks of Champions

Leadership, Access, and Advocacy
in the U.S. House of Representatives

Christine A. DeGregorio

Ann Arbor
The University of Michigan Press

Published in the United States of America by
The University of Michigan Press
Manufactured in the United States of America
⊚ Printed on acid-free paper

2000   1999   1998   1997   4   3   2   1

A CIP catalog record for this book is available from the British Library

Library of Congress Cataloging-in-Publication Data

DeGregorio, Christine A.

    Networks of champions : leadership, access, and advocacy in the U.S. House of Representatives / Christine A. DeGregorio.
      p. cm.
    Includes bibliographical references and index.
    ISBN 0-472-10762-3
    1. United States. Congress. House—Leadership.   2. Political leadership—United States.   3. Pressure groups—United States.
4. Lobbyists—United States.   5. United States—Politics and government—1981–1989.   I. Title.
JK1319.D44   1997
324'.4'092273—dc21   96-39404
                                                    CIP

for my mother and my father

Contents

Preface

This book examines what is noteworthy and unique about individuals in the U.S. House of Representatives who work often against incredible odds to win support for policies of great national importance. Because lawmaking is a team effort, moreover, the focus includes participants from different corners of the political stage. First and foremost are the officeholders who attract the attention of interested onlookers and the following of their voting colleagues. Next are professional, policy-minded staffers who, while accumulating expertise and credibility in their own right, quietly serve the interests and the reputations of their elected masters. Considered as well are scores of experienced advocates whose capacity to deliver desired policy outcomes to their principals rests initially on the success they achieve in reaching the leaders with a mind to hear and the power to accommodate their concerns.

For drawing my attention to the fact that issue leaders sometimes come from obscure stations within the institution and that lobbyists are in the business of ferreting them out before committing their own valuable resources to the fight, I am particularly indebted to Dr. Charls E. Walker of Charls E. Walker Associates, Inc. While well known and highly regarded in policy circles as a gifted economist and political consultant, for me and my students this talented man is a consummate educator. It was in a guest appearance on the American University campus that Dr. Walker shared with us his observations on the changes that have occurred in the House over the past thirty years and the implications the transformation holds for lobbyists and students of politics generally.

Power is no longer concentrated, he recalled from personal experience, as it was in the 1960s when rank-and-file legislators naturally complied with the wishes of a handful of party officials and committee chairs. Now the leaders are numerous. They shift from one stage in the legislative process to the next. And, more and more, they attract coalition partners with their substantive know-how and hard work, not simply with their authoritative titles.

This new, earned style of leadership that characterizes the modern House has important implications for practitioners and academics alike.

We are reminded, for example, that we have no idea what makes a leader different from a nonleader, nor of how large the leadership pool is once we account for the unranked individuals who enjoy a following for reasons other than formal position. We do not know because we have not asked. No studies of congressional leadership use as their starting point all members of the institution. In departing from common practice, I do just that. I identify House leaders on the basis of the firsthand observations of a random sample of 97 advocates who, in pressing their causes on Capitol Hill, make daily assessments of who is leading and who is following on a given issue.

The study participants also appraise the qualities of the individuals they identify, making it possible to test an explanatory model of leadership prominence that takes account of party label, seniority, and formal position, as well as more elusive traits like knowledge of the issues, interpersonal style, and political brinkmanship.

Implicit in Walker's discussion of what lobbyists look for in their leaders is the notion that not all leaders are equal and indeed that not all access is the same. The legislators with the position, expertise, and conviction it takes to shape a bill and mold support for passage may be the ones most hard-pressed to husband their time wisely, listening only to the most powerful outside groups. By identifying the combinations of leaders that advocates typically pursue, and by appraising the advocates' methods for securing access, this study addresses two additional aspects of political advocacy that are almost always missed.

First, conventional wisdom, which holds that citizen, cause-oriented groups are always outnumbered and outmuscled by occupation-oriented advocacy groups, has typically gone untested because of academics' proclivity to conduct either broad-based surveys or single case studies, approaches that are unequipped to control for the effects of different political environments. To attend to the omission, I observe the liaisons between leaders and lobbyists on six issues that are disparate in subject-matter complexity, scope of application, and public arousal. The evidence permits a systematic check on the extent to which particular types of advocacy organizations dominate in particular political settings.

Next, studies about Capitol Hill access focus almost exclusively on the connection between money, in particular campaign contributions from political action committees (PACs), and legislators' voting decisions. In the process, nonmonetary resources are almost always overlooked. In recognition of the ostensible value that these assets (e.g., expertise and grassroots support) hold for coalition builders in Congress, I ask advocates to reflect on the whole bundle of resources they use to reach leaders. Thus the evidence allows us to observe connections between *who* advocates work with in promoting their causes and *what* they offer their congressional partners to secure needed access.

I owe an enormous debt of gratitude to the busy individuals whose insights fill this book. Not only did they recall for me the players of merit on a given bill with which they were familiar, the advocates took the time to explain the special attributes that differentiated the named and unnamed officeholders and staff. As further evidence of the respondents' enthusiasm for the project and their openness in sharing hard-earned lessons about the travails of their profession, the participants took the time to offer many rules of thumb about how to locate helpful leaders and, once located, how to secure desired, ongoing access.

I am very grateful as well to a few dozen congressional staff members who reviewed numerous witness lists and helped me verify that I had uncovered all the advocates on the scene at the time. This task of detection was without a doubt the most tedious and least visible aspect of the inquiry. Yet the soundness of my findings relies in large measure on the patience and perspicacity with which the aides approached the work, at times even pulling out files, calendars, and rolodexes to make sure the job was done right.

In this six-year endeavor, I also learned to appreciate firsthand the quality of the American University's graduate students. In chronological order of their contributions, I am pleased to acknowledge in particular the help of Michael Koeppel, Kevin Snider, Stephanie Slocum, Marni Ezra, Julie Dolan, and Melissa Deckman. I took full advantage of their many talents and hope they learned as much from me as I did from them.

For their detailed comments on earlier drafts of the manuscript, I am especially grateful to Richard F. Fenno Jr., Barbara Sinclair, Leroy N. Rieselbach, Ronald G. Shaiko, William T. Bianco, and Charles D. Hadley. My colleagues at the American University provided numerous insights and valuable encouragement along the way. Candice J. Nelson, Susan W. Hammond, Laura I. Langbein, and James A. Thurber deserve special thanks. Neil Kerwin, the Dean of the School of Public Affairs, offered research funding that enabled me to remain focused. And the Dirksen Center for Congressional Research provided the seed money that launched the project. At the University of Michigan Press three individuals deserve special acknowledgment for the interest they took in my work and the assistance they provided at different junctures in the publication process—Malcolm Litchfield, Charles Myers, and Kevin Rennells.

I owe a tremendous personal debt to David Lalman, whose taste for politics is surpassed only by his love of words. The benefits I have reaped from countless hours in conversation with him on these subjects are

immeasurable. All awkward passages and mistakes are of course my own
to bear.

My parents, to whom this book is dedicated, are my personal champions. Through their example I have learned to value the truth and to look for it in uncommon places.

CHAPTER 1

Introduction

Congress is by design an adversarial place. Legislators represent constituents with vastly dissimilar expectations about what they want from government, and, as a consequence, policy deliberations often break down. It is so inevitable that conflicts will arise over matters about which people disagree and feel deeply that it is a wonder any major legislation ever attracts the approval of a majority of officeholders in the two chambers. That pronounced conflicts are overcome, as they eventually almost always are, is evidence to me that the institution has effective leaders who do what it takes to turn warring factions into winning coalitions.

This is a book about the leaders who emerge to champion policy in the face of adversity. It is an academic study that identifies leaders on the basis of the firsthand observations of 97 professional advocates who, in pressing their causes on Capitol Hill, are in the business of discerning leaders from followers in Congress. The study participants also assess the personal characteristics of the leaders they identify, and the accounts make it possible to estimate the extent to which leadership recognition rests on such factors as party affiliation, tenure in office, committee seat assignments, knowledge of the issues, and personal style. Because massive coalition efforts of the sorts examined here, moreover, involve several leaders, working from different vantage points within the institution, the study enlightens us about the size and composition of these multimember leadership networks.

Unlike most studies of congressional leadership, which restrict their attention to elected officials who possess the perquisites that come with formal rank (e.g., party leaders, committee and subcommittee chairs), I offer no preconditions. Anyone who commands the attention of the voting members of the institution is by my definition a leader. Thus the questions before us are new to political science inquiry: Who takes the lead on high-stakes policies that pass with difficulty? Do leaders possess attributes (sundry positions and personal talents) that nonleaders lack? Do issues that differ markedly in scope, visibility, and complexity, draw out different numbers and combinations of leaders who operate from different vantage points in the institution?

Moreover, it is abundantly clear from studies of congressional leadership that mustering the support needed to pass legislation of any consequence is not easy. On divisive issues, in particular, the stewards of a bill must trick, woo, and cajole their way to a following, and the job is too big for officeholders and their staff members to do without help. To succeed in building supportive voting blocs on controversial initiatives, astute leaders tap into a vast array of resources made available to them through professional advocates and organized interests. The resources include, for example, intricate analyses of policy alternatives, political intelligence about the electoral pressures under which undecided officeholders operate, targeted grass roots lobbying, money, and favorable media attention.

These and other resources, furthermore, serve the mutual interests of the leaders and the advocates. Just as lawmakers need the advocates to contribute sophisticated analyses, launch elaborate media campaigns, suggest alternative legislative language, and generally persevere in keeping initiatives alive, the advocates need the legislators to sponsor and promote their own legislative aims. The advocates need the lawmakers because in the final analysis, only officeholders can introduce, amend, and approve legislation. What is more, the advocates get noticed as they deliver the raw materials of power to the leaders of their choosing. And depending upon the leaders' assessments of the advocates' effectiveness in helping build the coalition, the advocates may receive substantial, ongoing access. When this access occurs, and it must be the objective of all determined lobbyists, they have a direct hand in constructing the laws of the nation.

While we are confident about the existence of these mutually advantageous relationships and their relevance to lawmaking, little certainty exists about the manner in which interested groups from different sectors within society parlay their own and their organizations' assets into Capitol Hill access.

Research on interest-group politics tells us that advocates hail from widely divergent settings in the pressure community and include fee-for-service lobbyists, union organizers, trade representatives, corporate executives, and citizen-based, cause-oriented advocates. Because most of the analysis disregards presidential appointees and bureaucrats, however, no comparisons are possible about the relative involvement of activists having public and private sponsorship. Also, while conventional wisdom suggests that the doors on Capitol Hill are more ajar to the promoters of business and industry, there are no tests of this claim across a variety of issues and conflicts.

Similarly, when it comes to knowing who leads and who follows within the institution, the information is patchy. Great strides have been made in understanding the way formal leaders of the political party hierarchies and committees use resources and rules to build support for their initiatives. Far less is known, however, about who takes the lead when this prominent elite remains on the sidelines of the debate or when power is seized from them, as it sometimes is, by legislators whose energy and force of ideas are sufficient to entice allegiance.

Because experience tells us that the narrow set of formally elected leaders underrepresents the full complement of individuals who contribute mightily to the passage of consequential policy, this study takes a comprehensive account of the players inside and outside the institution and assesses what contributes to their prominence. Also, by examining which types of promotional groups dominate on different issues and how they explain their access to Hill leaders, the evidence dispels some persistent mysteries about the policy-making process. In the end, we will be in a position to thoroughly evaluate three often repeated and as yet untested claims about leadership, access, and advocacy in the U.S. House of Representatives.

> *Claim 1:* While the institution theoretically adheres to the majoritarian principle, real power rests in the hands of a small covey of elected leaders (party bosses and committee barons) who dictate the solutions for others to follow.
>
> *Claim 2:* Representatives abrogate the responsibilities for lawmaking that citizens entrust with them by deferring too often to experts among their staff and special-interest organizations.
>
> *Claim 3:* Unequal access translates into unequal influence, and members of Congress open their doors the widest to the monied crowd from corporate America.

The evidence for this study comes from interviews with 97 advocates, who, through active firsthand participation in the policy process, learned which individuals inside Congress figured prominently in shepherding six bills to final passage. The policies, disparate in subject matter and scope but uniformly serious in their consequences to the country, include: Contra aid (H.J.R. 523), farm credit reform (H.R. 3030), omnibus drug (H.R. 5210), nuclear testing limitations (Section 924 of H.R. 4264), omnibus trade (H.R. 4848), and welfare reform (H.R. 1720).

Owing in part to the originality of this investigative approach, this study redefines congressional leadership as we know it. First, the inventory of leaders includes some obscure individuals who until now went unnoticed because they hold no formal rank within either the party or the committee hierarchies, the conventional method of identifying congressional leaders. Second, by comparing the attributes of leaders and nonleaders, a new picture comes into focus. No less important than formal rank in the chamber are several other characteristics that attend having a reputation of prominence. Included among these ingredients for leadership are knowledge of the subject matter, experience in the chamber, a facility for bargaining and compromise, the right committee assignments, and commitment to hard work.

The inventory of promotional organizations is also varied, including intergovernmental agencies, private corporations, trade and professional associations, for-profit lobbying firms, and citizen cause-oriented groups. Two findings are of particular interest here. First, the types of groups that numerically dominate the advocacy scene differ with the salience and complexity of the issues under consideration. Second, promotional organizations possess different bundles of resources, and where campaign finance or the size of one's membership base gains access in one instance, personal experience and knowledge of the issues do so in the next. So organizations that cannot buy access with donations can gain access nonetheless with information and credibility, assets that are highly valued by leaders who are in the business of building support for divisive issues.

The new and more accurate map of the leadership and advocacy terrain serves both positive and normative purposes. Not only do we arrive at better descriptions of and explanations for the breadth of the elaborate and mutually reinforcing partnerships that prevail in designing legislation, but also we uncover disparities in the opportunities different participants have to take part in the back-and-forth negotiations that occur.

A word or two on terminology is in order. The *advocates* are the study participants whose expert judgments inform us on whom the voting membership in the House looks to for leadership. When I identify *leaders* and *followers,* I am speaking only of the players inside the U.S. House of Representatives. And whereas the term *leaders* may include both officeholders and aides, according to their capacities for building majorities, the term *followers* includes only officeholders whose votes count in determining the success or failure of a legislative initiative. Anyone who is not a leader is, by implication, a follower.

The Focus of the Study

My aim in writing this book is to explain the workings of House leadership in a way that is practical as well as theoretically useful. Academics, legislators, and lobbyists should be able to use the findings to their advantage. Legislators and lobbyists, who are interested in building coalitions to secure policies, no less than scholars interested in better foundations for their theories, should find value in the descriptions of leadership networks and the avenues of power in the modern House. As I have argued, legislators need advocates just as advocates need legislators to achieve their policy goals. Thus, I examine leadership and advocacy as two sides of one coin. Networks of access—who works with whom on a regular basis in developing public policy—vary remarkably depending on the participants, their resources, and the issue areas involved. These relationships and their implications for political behavior will be outlined briefly, starting with leadership.

Leadership

Most studies of congressional leadership focus on particular individuals or groups of individuals because of the titles they hold in the institution. David Rohde (1991), Barbara Sinclair (1983), Charles O. Jones (1970, 1968), and Randall Ripley (1969, 1967) exemplify this tradition in their explorations of the many dimensions of House leadership from the perspective of its parties' two most visible players—the Speaker and the minority leader. Other scholars offer a more decentralized view of House leadership and examine instead those who head up congressional committees and subcommittees. Examples of this perspective include the work of Richard L. Hall (1992), Charles L. Evans (1990), Steven S. Smith and Christopher J. Deering (1990), Randall Strahan (1990), Joseph K. Unekis and Leroy N. Rieselbach (1983), and Richard Fenno (1973).

Despite differences in approaches, the conclusion of these two methodological approaches and foci is the same. Leadership and followership are considered features of the same dynamic. Followers attach themselves to particular leaders because they have confidence that these chosen leaders will take them where they want to go. In addition, three themes recur with extraordinary regularity in explaining the effectiveness of leaders. First, formal leaders hold positions that offer visibility and privilege. Second, it is easier to win support by trading off something of value for the desired vote than it is to secure compliance from authoritative command. This is to say that personal talents for sizing up people and knowing when and when not to compromise are as crucial to the influence game as is position with its accompanying privileges. Third, the informal powers of persuasion that succeed in building support change constantly with changes in the circumstances and the targets of one's influence.

When studies of congressional leadership explain variations in power—focusing, as they do, exclusively on the *established* leaders' capacities for building compliance with their wishes—we never hear about the individuals who have attentive followers for reasons other than being the head of a party or the head of a committee. How commonplace is it that leaders attract followers by unconventional means? And if position retains its distinction as a key ingredient to power, what is the relative value, in terms of attracting followers, of different kinds of positions? Do individuals who head up prominent committees have the same leadership appeal as those holding high-level posts in either of the two formal party hierarchies?

To date, we have no answers to these questions because we lack an inventory of leadership that starts with a method of identification other than institutional position. This is the challenge. Here we identify the leaders by asking participants close to the action to distinguish for us the players of consequence from the bystanders. Then, with the leaders delineated in this way, we examine the relative value that an array of institutional positions, personal characteristics, and contextual circumstances bring to bear on one's leadership recognition.

Advocacy

Our republican form of democracy calls for an attentive citizenry that will express its likes and dislikes not just episodically at election time but throughout the year. According to John Meuller, it is the right to criticize elected officials that truly energizes democratic governments. In his words:

> [I]f citizens have the right to complain, to petition, to organize, to protest, to demonstrate, to strike, to threaten to emigrate, to shout, to publish, to express a lack of confidence, to bribe, and to wheedle in back corridors, government will tend to respond to the sounds of the shouters and the importunings of the wheedlers; that is, it will necessarily become responsive whether there are elections or not. (1992, 984)

He is making two points here. The first is a matter of some dispute:[1] The capacity to organize against one's government is more important than the capacity to vote. On the second point there is little disagreement: Government is most responsive to those who shout the loudest. Indeed, most students of protest are interested in their subject as much to keep score of who wins and who loses as to understand who complains and why (J. Walker 1991, Pertschuk and Schaetzel 1989, Cigler and Loomis 1986).

Petitions come from a pressure community that is made up of individual citizens and organized groups, and interest-group scholars devote the majority of their attention to the groups. Theories about organized advocacy range from explaining why groups form to the ways they go about influencing government. The investigators usually adopt one of three approaches. Those following the first approach examine the origins, composition, resources, missions, and strategies of a single organization (e.g., Common Cause, the Sierra Club, and the American Agricultural Movement, Inc.). For excellent examples of this case-study approach, see the work of Lawrence S. Rothenberg (1992), Candice J. Nelson (1994), and Allan J. Cigler (1986). Another circle of scholars takes the second approach and examines the resources, strategies, and networking, if any, that occur among groups that organize around a single cause (e.g., agriculture, welfare, environment, or human rights). The work of Christopher J. Bosso (1991), Diana M. Evans (1991), Alissa Rubin (1991), and William P. Browne (1986) adeptly illustrates this approach. Alternatively, employing an institutional rather than a policy focus, investigators taking the third approach examine the entire interest-group community. Jack L. Walker (1991) and Kay Lehman Schlozman and John T. Tierney (1986) profitably use this tactic to compare the ways groups with different resources and missions establish, maintain, and insinuate themselves in the struggle for power.

The current study merges the policy focus and the institutional focus by examining the characteristics of a wide array of groups that promote their points of view around selected policies. This approach provides an uncommon opportunity to compare how organizationally dissimilar groups (public and private, profit and nonprofit) acting within the same policy domain go about selecting leaders and gaining desired access and how different issues correspond with dissimilarly skewed promotional communities.

To push the comparison further, I expand the definition of a pressure community to include representatives from the executive branch of government. These individuals, presidential appointees and high-level bureaucrats, urge legislators every day to embrace presidential initiatives and to pass policy that advances the chief executive's agenda. In so doing, they compete directly with private-sector lobbyists for time with and sway over the lawmakers. Because of the predilection of academics to study either legislative-executive relations or legislative–interest-group relations, we are typically prevented from comparing how the advocates from the two arenas approach House policy champions. This study provides just such an opening.

Access

Hinging the identification of who is and who is not a leader on the observations of the advocates makes it essential that we elicit opinions from a broad cross section of participants in the interest-group community who are sufficiently close to the action to observe and report it accurately. The sampling scheme, delineated in appendix 1, explicitly addresses these concerns. Here, we take comfort in observing simply that the study participants rarely experience being denied access to prestigious members of the leadership elite in the House. Had the acknowledged heavy hitters (i.e., high-ranking party leaders and committee chairs) turned away from the advocates, we would have to question the advocates' depiction of events. Instead, the openness with which House members received the outsiders helps allay the fear that the real leaders operate somewhere out of view.

Easy accessibility speaks well of the lawmakers' readiness to work with the committed advocates who appear on the policy horizon. Before we can conclude that access is equitably distributed to all who apply, however, we need to examine the mutual selection process that occurs on the way to establishing these leader-advocate partnerships.

My expectations of the attachments that form between pairs of advocates and leaders are informed by the insights of numerous scholars who have been working in two subfields of American politics: legislative behavior and interest-group politics. Like them, I accept the basic assumption that all human endeavor is rational. The perspective is not very demanding. It merely necessitates that individuals have the capacity to know their own likes and dislikes and to make commonsense assessments of what will and will not satisfy their interests. The outlook is well suited for studying advocates' access to congressional leaders because it acknowledges the voluntary and mutual nature of the relationships in question. Beyond the fact that the congressional leaders want to succeed in passing policy and need the House votes to do it, they work under enormous time constraints. In circumstances like these, the rational thing for legislators to do is be selective about whom they give substantial access to. The advocates, for their part, know the pressures under which the issue leaders operate, and they secure access by giving the leaders something of value in return for time. Because leaders come to the policy battle with different assets and liabilities, clever advocates must discern these needs and proffer their own resources accordingly.

Several testable propositions stem from this reasoning. First, I expect professional advocates to work with different numbers of leaders. Those with ample stores of time, connections, insights, and analyses will be advantaged over their competitors who have limited amounts of each. Second, I expect that differences in the composition of advocates' leadership networks (the proportion of officeholders to aides or the proportion of veterans to newcomers) depend in part on the advocates' personal qualities (their prior experience and contacts), the resources of their organizational sponsors (membership size, budgets, and staff), and the political contexts within which they seek congressional access.

Last, the findings about access, more than any other concepts with which we are dealing, raise questions about fairness and equity. While it is not my intention to compare the relative influence that groups have on House decisions, it stands to reason that, for example, those who meet with 44 officeholders are getting something different for their efforts than are their colleagues who meet with two officeholders and three aides. From this perspective, the data on who works with whom address a normative question about access and influence in Washington.

The Approach

Figure 1.1 provides a schematic depiction of the key ingredients of this research design. Centered at the bottom are six selected policies that fairly accurately represent the scope and complexity of the issue challenges that befit the modern Congress. Whereas most initiatives of any consequence die in committee rooms, never even making it to the floor, these bills survived successive rounds of scrutiny and gained passage on the chamber floor. The achievement redounds to two types of officeholders: (1) the followers, who, for whatever reasons, are content to go along with the policy arrangement before them, and (2) the leaders, who I theorize have the requisite balance of position and talent to assemble voting majorities at key junctures in the life of a bill. These leaders are the policy champions, and they include both legislators and unelected professional staff. Last are the interested advocates, an eclectic group of activists from different institutional settings, who organize to promote their visions of good policy. These advocates are the study participants who supply the insights for the analysis.

My decision to narrow the search for policy champions, first to the U.S. House of Representatives and second to a handful of bills considered during the 100th Congress, has obvious strengths and weaknesses. In my view, the benefits that accrue from ratcheting down the research focus more than outweigh the costs of learning nothing about leadership in the Senate. The reasoning for this and other methodological decisions follows.

The Context: The Institution and the Issues

When there are many competing explanations for the same behavior, as there are in the study of congressional leadership, the only way to make any sense out of the confusing hodgepodge of circumstances is to

ADVOCATES	CHAMPIONS
(Study Participants)	Leaders
	(Officeholders and Aides)

Followers
(Officeholders)

SELECTED POLICIES

Contra	Omnibus	Farm	Nuclear	Omnibus	Welfare
Aid	Drug	Credit	Test Ban	Trade	Reform

Fig. 1.1. Schematic depiction of the issues and the multiple roles of key players

artificially reduce what is allowed to vary. By focusing on the House and not the Senate, we place all 435 officeholders on an even footing with respect to (1) the organizational environment within which they operate, (2) their election cycles (every two years), and (3) the size of their constituencies. Knowing that these features are the same for everyone, we can dismiss them as explanatory causes of leadership and focus instead on several of the remaining factors that distinguish legislators—their years in office, electoral vulnerability, committee assignments, elected leadership positions, substantive expertise, political savvy, affability, and accessibility.[2]

Next, from the foregoing discussion of leadership, we know that context matters. Limiting the investigation to one Congress fixes the players and their positions, and to some extent their opponents, over the two-year period. When the session began on January 3, 1987, the Democrats held a 258–177 majority over the Republicans—no change from the previous Congress. For the first time in six years, the Democrats had regained control of the Senate. And at the other end of Pennsylvania Avenue they faced a somewhat weakened president. Republican Ronald Reagan, who had been a formidable threat during his early years in office, was now entering the lame-duck period of his second term. What is more, he had been politically damaged by reports that his administration had been involved in selling arms to Iran and funneling the profits to the Nicaraguan Contras.[3]

For two reasons in particular I chose the 100th Congress (1987–88). At the time that I was beginning to tackle this project, the action had just come to a close around the passage of several major policies, and memories were fresh in the minds of those who participated. Second, had the conflicts over welfare reform, trade, and antidrug policy ended in a stalemate as did the amendments to the Clean Air Act, I would have no leadership successes to ponder. Instead, the period had relevancy. Many policy champions found the wherewithal to hammer out the passage of several controversial and broad-gauged policies.

Because House members specialize in and gain credibility and influence over some policy areas and not others, any study of leadership must take into account the breadth of the congressional agenda (Rohde 1991; B. Sinclair 1995, 1983; Ripley 1983; Cooper and Brady 1981). Change the issues and you are likely to get different leaders. To guard against this unwanted confusion, I restricted the focus to six consequential and substantively diverse bills.[4] Moreover, because much of the early legislative work is done in committee, I was careful to choose bills that went to a wide cross section of panels, ensuring that everyone, regardless of committee affiliation, has the opportunity to appear on the leadership radar screen. See appendix 1 for elaboration on the selection of the issues.

There is wisdom in observing the leadership and followership that emerges around the formulation of specific policies for other reasons as well. The issues not only center attention around tangible and memorable events (e.g., hearings, markups, votes), but they also provide different substantive challenges and different political contexts. Without ensuring that complexity and scope of the policies vary, for example, how can we observe for these effects on leadership and advocacy? So while the study design focuses on little more than a handful of issues, those selected represent a reasonable range of the challenges that call for leadership in Congress. These are also the concerns that typically evoke widespread promotional campaigns on the part of myriad organized groups.

The overhaul of the nation's welfare system (H.R. 1720), for example, was one of the 100th Congress's most significant achievements. The final version of H.R. 1720 provided for $3.34 billion to strengthen child support, provide educational benefits to adult welfare recipients, and require states to extend benefits to poor two-parent families.

Certainly one of the most lauded accomplishments was the passage of the antidrug bill (H.R. 5210), which called for the appointment of a cabinet-level "drug czar," more stringent penalties for drug dealers and addicts, and additional programs for the treatment and rehabilitation of drug addicts. After dropping or modifying most of the controversial elements of the package, the House passed H.R. 5210 on October 21, 1988, with overwhelming bipartisan support (346–11: R 150–0; D 196–11) (Lawrence 1988).

Concern over international trade policy grew throughout the 1980s as the unrelenting trade deficit hounded American business and industry. Lawmakers agreed on the end—"fair" trade to stimulate American markets abroad—but they differed on the means. Some advocated protectionist solutions, and others promoted free trade. After a three-year odyssey marked more by technical morass than by high drama, the final version of the Omnibus Trade and Competitiveness Act of 1988 (H.R. 4848) passed easily and with little fanfare (Wehr 1988).

The instability of the farmer cooperatives, known as the Farm Credit System (FCS), had eluded earlier government fixes in 1985 and 1986. Depressed farm prices and steeply declining agricultural land values created a record number of defaulted loans. In 1987 the problem had finally reached catastrophic proportions. The window of opportunity had opened for reform, and everything was on the table. H.R. 3030 had it all. There were ideological disagreements over the size and nature of the bailout and the scope of the administrative restructuring. There were turf fights among congressional committees and hard feelings over the haste with which Speaker Jim Wright wanted to conclude the action. All in all, after much negotiation and compromise, everyone came out a winner.

Two additional issues had the quality of never letting go. The first, limiting tests of nuclear weapons, has become a congressional rite of passage. The 100th Congress was no exception. As in previous years, test-ban legislation won in the House and lost in the Senate. This is the only issue under study that failed to produce statutory guidelines for governmental action. Nonetheless, House passage of Section 924 of the Defense Authorization Act (H.R. 4264) that limited nuclear testing to 1 kiloton was considered to be a policy success by many within the antitesting community.

Second, Congress rejected in February and awarded in March 1988 aid to the Contras, guerrillas fighting the leftist government in Nicaragua.[5] Although the peace agreement had been signed earlier in the month between the Contras and the Nicaraguan government, these funds were meant to help victims of the seven-year conflict and hold the Contras together in case the negotiated settlement failed and until the new administration in Washington put together its own policy toward the region. Assistance to Central America (H.R. 523) was one of a six-year series of votes pertaining to the contras, and more than any other issue under investigation here, this decision turned most vehemently on party politics.

Table 1.1 summarizes the key elements of the six issues on political and substantive grounds. A content analysis of news reports at the time indicates clear differences across issues. Those with international implications include nuclear testing, Contra aid, and omnibus trade. Welfare reform is a peculiarly domestic issue. Farm credit and antidrug policies, however, straddle the domestic and international arenas.

The issues also aroused different sorts of disagreements. Some debates were primarily ideological, turning on core values about what properly remains in the public and private domains. Other issues were

TABLE 1.1   Comparative Analysis of Selected Legislation by Key Factors

	Contra Aid (H.J.R. 523)	Omnibus Drug (H.R. 5210)	Issues (Bill Numbers) Farm Credit (H.R. 3030)	Nuclear Test Ban (H.R. 4264)	Omnibus Trade (H.R. 4848)	Welfare Reform (H.R. 1720)
			Key Factors			
Policy Domain[a]						
Arena	Internat'l	Mixed	Mixed	Internat'l	Internat'l	Domestic
Complexity	Low	Low	High	High	High	Low
Scope	Narrow	Broad	Narrow	Narrow	Broad	Broad
Cost						
Senate	17.7 M	2.8 B	4.0 B	n.a.[b]	5.5 B	5.9 B
House	17.7 M	2.1 B	2.5 B		5.0 B	4.0 B
Political Context[a]						
Conflict	High	High	High	High	High	High
Salience	High	Low	Low	Low	High	Low

[a]See the text for an explanation of these concepts.

[b] The provision to limit nuclear tests to one kiloton appeared as a section (624) of the Defense Authorization Act (1988). While the entire appropriation was large (not included here), the regulation was costless and not a salient feature of the debate.

technically complex, with their controversies centered primarily on grounds of what is feasible. Of the mix, contra aid and welfare reform fall most squarely in the first category, whereas nuclear testing, omnibus trade, and farm credit fall predominantly in the latter category. While the drug bill entailed discussions about the feasibility of protecting our sprawling borders from the flow of illegal drugs, discourse primarily turned on moral questions such as the appropriateness of subjecting federal employees to random drug tests.

Legislative initiatives have broad and narrow applications (scope) as well, depending on who is affected by the promised outcomes. With this application criterion in mind, the policies affecting the smallest clientele are Contra aid, farm credit reform, and the nuclear test ban.[6] Welfare reform, omnibus drug, and omnibus trade reach successively larger populations.[7]

Policy debates also occur in a context. Depending on many factors that are external to the issue itself (e.g., bitterness held over from a previous fight, election time, high unemployment), the deliberations may be rancorous or harmonious. They may attract a lot of mass interest or hardly any at all. And these conditions—conflict and public salience—facilitate some leaders and advocates and hinder others.

Every policy selected for consideration here drew substantial conflict. With the exception of Contra aid and omnibus trade, however, the battles were fairly narrowly circumscribed. On these two issues, the Democratic party leadership in Congress took a strident position and battled with the administration, intensifying the conflict and extending the visibility of these issues beyond Capitol Hill. Presidential campaign politics also magnified the antagonism. Interbranch fighting became particularly severe over a protectionist provision in H.R. 4848, championed by presidential hopeful Richard Gephardt (D-Missouri).[8]

The plight of the farmers received some public attention through such cinematic box-office hits as *Country,* but in general the issue interested only those individuals who were personally affected—farmers and ranchers, bankers and insurance companies.[9] The negotiations over nuclear testing were the most obscure of the six issues, probably because of the technical complexity of the bill's provisions. In contrast, the omnibus drug bill probably drew little notice in the media, because of the speed with which it went through Congress, about a month.[10]

To some extent, the subject matter of an issue and its political context are linked. Issues that are impenetrable for ordinary citizens usually arouse little attention. Those that promise to help (or threaten to hurt) large segments of society may also be the policies that arouse mass interest. Even if it is sometimes difficult to disentangle these characteristics of the policies, they warrant discussion because they likely affect which leaders and which advocates decide to get involved.

The Advocates

To determine which House members took the lead on these six policies, I asked a randomly selected group of advocates who had a great deal at stake in the outcomes. I included in the group presidential appointees, bureaucrats, fee-for-service lobbyists, and other professionals who worked behind the scenes promoting their particular points of view.

For two reasons, my construction of *advocate* is broader than that used in most textbook definitions. First, for decades presidents and their lobbyists have done informally what this study does scientifically: identify those individuals in Congress who, owing to their positions, the forcefulness of their ideas, their tactical prowess, and other such skills, seize for themselves a central role in lawmaking (Neustadt 1990, Kernell 1986). Because top government executives compete for favorable attention from the legislative leaders just as other advocates do, and given their knowledge of what goes on behind the scenes, politically, this inquiry would be remiss to omit them.

Second, because most political scientists specialize in studying either the byplay between the administration and the Congress *or* that between interest-group representatives and the Congress, we rarely have a chance to compare the political networking of the two arenas at once. The evidence serves to fill an intellectual void and further justifies the inclusion of presidential aides. Excluded from the definition of advocates are the neutral experts (e.g., university professors) who limit their involvement to contributing background information and analyses for informal briefings and public testimony.

The fact that legislators routinely reach out to interested advocates to brief them on the substantive merits as well as the political ramifications of embracing this or that position makes the advocates excellent firsthand witnesses of the players and the events.[11] In addition and perhaps more important, the advocates make good judges because they size up the leadership capabilities of officeholders day in, day out. The incentives to do so are varied. The advocates are typically experts who spend their entire workdays on the one narrow issue that Congress has now put on the national agenda for review. They, or the principal to whom they are accountable, care deeply about the outcome. Furthermore, as is customary in most organizations (even the federal bureaucracy), they operate with limited resources. There is never enough time to see and "educate" all 435 representatives with the "correct" interpretation of facts. As a consequence, advocates have every incentive to work closely with the "fewest" number of individuals, those who will corral the greater number of votes.

The selection of advocates to participate in the study is as important to the accuracy of the results as the choice of issues. The three-step sampling strategy that I used to guard against distortions is summarized in appendix 1. As I demonstrate there, the participants closely resemble the distribution of groups that typically comprise the pressure group community writ large.

The Instrument

I talked with each study participant for an average of 60 minutes either in person or, in cases of distance, by telephone. The initial questions pertaining to the advocates, their organizational affiliations, and their objectives served to break the ice and screen participants for their appropriateness to the study.[12] After assessing the extent to which the participants achieved their organizations' policy interests, they identified, by name, everyone in their leadership networks. The interview protocol instructed them to omit mentioning the House insiders they lobbied for a single vote and, instead, to name only the special few leaders whose help they sought because these leaders have an inside following (i.e., "other House members look to them for giving voting cues and for building coalitions"). In response to this question, each respondent named from two to 44 leaders. And while the question makes no special mention of congressional aides, many study participants thought it appropriate and necessary to include them in their tally of leaders.

This and the follow-up question that called upon the interviewees to assess the personal qualifications of each individual they listed took the bulk of the interview time. The study participants evaluated every leader as possessing or not possessing several qualifications from a prepared list of attributes.[13] Was a particular leader included in the advocate's network, for example, because she or he was a member of the "party leadership" or a member of a "committee" with jurisdiction over the bill? Was the leader selected because of her or his "special subject-matter expertise," "political savvy," "accessibility," or "affability"? When the respondents completed this assessment, they were invited to include additional qualities not provided on the list. After evaluating the attributes of the leaders, the respondents then reflected on their own (e.g., former member of Congress, prior experience advocating on this issue) and their organizations' characteristics (e.g., size, credibility, affiliated political action committee). The session ended with several more open-ended questions about the lessons they learned that could be applied to future lobbying campaigns. The interview questionnaire is provided in appendix 2.

Overview

Members of Congress have two main functions: to make laws and to represent their constituents. Because the two are frequently in conflict with one another (deliberation and compromise often run counter to district attentiveness), the coalitions that are needed to pass major legislation come together infrequently and with great difficulty. It takes a rare blend of leadership and followership for one legislative initiative to prevail, particularly when the stakes are high and the competition of ideas is stiff.

Until now, students of congressional leadership have examined only one narrow band of leaders, those in highly visible party and committee positions. Their findings, while rich with insights on the transfer of power from one formal leader to the next and the mechanisms used to attract compliant followers, are blind to the power brokers and coalition builders who come from other less visible corners of the institution. Who makes up this larger, more complete rendering of the leadership sphere, and what separates them from the rest? Chapter 2 addresses these questions after first providing the intellectual arguments and background information needed for analyzing how power becomes stratified in the U.S. House of Representatives.

The evidence from this investigation provides several new insights about congressional leadership. First, of the 383 individuals who achieve recognition as leaders, 36 percent are unelected professional staff. While this finding appears to play into the hands of the critics who say that staff are too powerful and undermine the representative nature of the institution, other findings counter this simplistic conclusion. Nine out of ten aides who figure among the leadership elite, for example, operate in conjunction with and under the direction of elected officials who are themselves identified as leaders. Staff, more than their elected counterparts, also play specialist roles. Among the generalists who emerge as leaders over an array of diverse issues, the unelected barely appear. What is more, the elected leaders are no less equipped than their aides to negotiate the fine points of the issues. Indeed, according to the study participants, the legislators score higher than their aides do on two of the studied attributes that correspond with leadership—substantive expertise and political savvy.

Chapter 3 focuses on the advocates and their organizations after first taking stock of several important theories that help explain the behavior of interest groups and bureaucracies. From this intellectual heritage we know to expect a sizable number of participants, with a possible skew in the direction of organizational wealth and political patronage—two ingredients necessary for fledgling promotional enterprises to mature (Rosenstone and Hansen 1993, J. Walker 1991, Salisbury 1990). Because scholars seldom compare the organizational makeup of pressure-group communities across diverse policy domains, we have no way of knowing how accurate this picture is from one issue to the next. A second blind spot in our understanding of advocacy has to do with the role of government officials. Are they more or less numerous than lobbyists from nongovernmental interest groups? And within the public sector, who dominates, federal agents or state and local representatives? Until we can answer these questions with some degree of precision, we are incapable of explaining who gets what from government and why.

The evidence from this chapter begins to tell the story, not all of which comports with conventional wisdom. For example, for-profit organizations sponsored by business and industry do not dominate promotional politics across the board. And while occupational organizations, in particular nonprofit professional and trade associations, make up the largest share of the interest-group community in almost every case, citizen cause-oriented groups have their day. These promotional entities, which are bound by a common cause rather than a workplace or occupation, outnumber the rest when issues are salient to the mass public and when the subject matter is not technically complex. Both of these phenomena occurred in the battle that ensued over funding the Contras in Nicaragua, and the citizen groups dominated the scene.

Within the public sector, administration officials are most abundant when the president's autonomy is questioned. This situation occurred with the Omnibus Trade and Competitive Act of 1988 (H.R. 4848). State and local officials, together with their professional and trade associations (e.g., the National Governors Association, the American Public Welfare Association) eclipse administration officials when policies threaten to alter current governmental arrangements for funding and authority. Welfare reform and omnibus drug legislation engaged sizable numbers of advocates from these governmental jurisdictions.

In keeping with their need to conserve resources and develop credibility over narrow areas of specialization, advocacy organizations rarely launch full-scale promotional campaigns over disparate causes. And so it is with the participating organizations. Fewer than 10 percent of the groups lobbied Congress on more than one of the six issues. And when organizations collaborate with one another, their coalitions are informal arrangements that serve temporary mutual interests. More often than not, what is at stake is a matter of economic and political interest—jobs and the authority to distribute rights and resources in society.

Chapter 4 focuses on the networks between the advocates and the leaders. Here, the theories from legislative and interest-group politics point to the importance of personal ambition. Influence-seeking leaders use formal and informal powers to piece together the desired number of House votes. To be successful, these coalition builders need information on the preferences of their would-be followers and ample utilitarian benefits with which to woo compliance. The advocates, in turn, anticipate the leaders' needs for resources (e.g., information, money, contacts) and offer goods and services in exchange for access and the influence that it may bear. From this rational choice perspective, we expect resources to matter a great deal in determining who meets with whom in the promotion of policy.

Once again the evidence is mixed, for while there is a substantial disparity in the resources that organizations have to distribute in exchange for access, the inequity has little bearing on the advocates' ties to Congress. The leaders' names may vary, but their positions and parties do not. On average, all advocates reported having a similarly diversified array of policy champions: Democrats exceeded Republicans, committee leaders exceeded party leaders, and officeholders exceeded staff.

The story becomes even more complex when one compares the lobbyists' assessments of what opens doors for them in Congress. We find, for example, that the advocates, while similarly resourceful in capitalizing on their strengths, rely on different personal and organizational assets. Advocates from for-profit occupational groups such as AT&T and American Express stressed the importance of their personal credibility and their issue expertise. In contrast, those from occupational nonprofits such as the International Ladies Garment Workers' Union and the National Association of Manufacturers, first and foremost highlighted the size of their memberships and their organizations' credibility. Representatives from citizen groups such as the American Civil Liberties Union and Council for a Livable World stressed their issue expertise and their professional service. Thus, there is more to political influence than money and contacts. Busy legislative leaders may want something for their time, but the something is more varied than simple campaign contributions. It includes vigilance, expertise, and hard work.

Next, there is a relationship between what advocates use to open doors on Capitol Hill and whose doors they open. The organizations with above-average memberships cited disproportionately more officeholders than aides in their leadership networks. Advocates who provide in-kind services (e.g., writing speeches or issue briefs) in return for access included among their champions more Democrats than Republicans and more staff members than officeholders. Administration officials are distinct from other lobbyists in that they have formal ties to certain congressional committees by virtue of their executive jurisdictions. Accordingly, these participants relied almost exclusively on their governmental positions to gain the access they needed. Furthermore, to no one's surprise, lobbyists for the Republican White House identified nearly as many Republican as Democratic leaders in Congress. This report is markedly more bipartisan than that of the advocates from private-sector organizations, who included 75 percent (occupational groups) to 84 percent (citizen groups) Democrats, respectively. Also, administration advocates included fewer aides in their leadership networks than did other participants: 20 percent as opposed to 30 percent, respectively.

The two types of federal employees permit one additional comparison about which we know very little. To what extent do career civil servants operate differently from presidential appointees in their dealings with congressional leaders? As they describe it, the bureaucrats do not "choose" who they work with at all. They simply respond to every request they receive for information and advice, regardless of the requester's party, status, seniority, competence, and policy perspective. The civil servants are not strategic in discerning the leaders and the followers, and the complexion of their networks reflects their lack of discrimination. Presidential appointees are another matter. They operate like the nongovernmental advocates, devoting time to the special few members whom others look to in the House for competent leadership. While this distinction in professional styles corresponds with known differences in these employees' work orientations, there are sufficiently few comparative studies such as this to make the finding noteworthy.

Besides analyzing the extent to which advocate-leader liaisons vary from one organizational setting to another, chapter 4 tackles the question of equity head-on. Advocates report on a scale of zero to 100 points, with 100 being a perfect fit, the extent to which the policy outcomes resemble their ideal preferences. Notwithstanding the difficulties inherent in self-reporting satisfaction (Sudman and Bradburn 1982, Backstrom and Cesar 1981), the data provide some interesting results. While the advocates generally give high praise for the legislators' handiwork, the most satisfied (nonprofits) and the least satisfied (administration) participants work with the highest concentration of officeholders. From this ironic result I contend that how close the advocates come to realizing their goals has more to do with the distance they mean to travel in the policy space than whom they align with in Congress. Just as spending a lot of money in a congressional race may beckon electoral vulnerability, working with the most prominent leaders in Congress may signal trouble in a policy debate.

The final chapter assembles the findings on leadership, advocacy, and access in the U.S. House of Representatives, with an eye toward the future. Since the days of the 100th Congress, much has changed and much has remained the same in terms of the House's membership, institutional structure, and policy environment.

For the first time in forty years, the Republican party in 1995 took formal control of the chamber, having won a narrow majority of seats in the previous November election (230 Republicans, 204 Democrats, 1 Independent).[14] What is more, this is no mere change in personnel. Along with several procedural and staffing changes that will no doubt affect the process and the players, the solutions that are now being debated represent a distinct ideological shift toward less government intervention and more local control.

Continuities abound as well, however, and they will condition what happens over the foreseeable future. A sizable proportion (47.6 percent) of the current House membership (before November 1996 elections) were present at the time of the study. Of the number holding formal rank within the party and committee hierarchies, 88.1 percent were in office during the time of the study, and 44.6 percent of them were properly identified as leaders by the study participants in the late 1980s.

Congressional committees, the institutional location where most bills are formulated and refined, still provide the best vantage points for demonstrating commitment to the issues, subject matter expertise, and strategic prowess, the attributes that cultivate leadership appeal. And measures to reform welfare, reduce crime and drugs, stimulate trade and the economy, provide for the health care of all Americans, and secure global peace are massive undertakings that will occupy clever decision makers for some time to come. Furthermore, the scope, salience, and complexity of these concerns will necessitate creative, enduring partnerships between issue leaders and advocates. Hence, the chapter provides several guideposts for future academic inquiry as well as some practical rules of thumb to help leaders and advocates maximize their individual and joint endeavors in the production of our nation's laws.

CHAPTER 2

The Champions: Mapping the Leadership Terrain

Beyond being on the right side of the issue and having a strong coalition of supporters outside Congress, on the inside you need a '*good horse.*' A good horse is good on substance. He knows the intricacies of the issue. Also, he knows when and when not to compromise. If you can find someone who is good on the issues and the politics of course you want both.

—Charls E. Walker

In this excerpt from his 1989 address on how to lobby Congress, prominent Washington consultant Charls E. Walker advises his audience on two central points.[1] First, if advocates are to acquire power on Capitol Hill, they need allies inside the institution who are willing to work with them in promoting the issues the advocates care about. Second, not just any ally will do. The advocates need to be selective about who they choose to take up their causes. Walker stresses the personal over the structural side of power. The only individuals with any promise of securing passage of a bill are those who are well versed on both the subject matter and the politics of the issue. Furthermore, because power is so diffused within the institution, several individuals often share leadership responsibilities, operating as if in a relay race, passing the torch among themselves at critical junctures.

In discerning the leaders from the nonleaders, the advocates conduct the same type of analysis that voting members of the House engage in when they search for competent individuals to push the policies they want passed. This is because compliance is voluntary, and officeholders go along with leaders only when it is in the followers' interest to do so. Thus, for certain individuals to be selected by their colleagues to fulfill leadership functions, the would-be leaders must have the wherewithal to arouse expectations of competence. This construction of how influence works is not only consistent with the accomplishments of political scientists who have studied widely in the area (Rohde 1991, Neustadt 1990, B. Jones 1989, C. Jones 1988, B. Sinclair 1983, Mackaman 1981, Peabody 1976), it comports well with most general definitions of leadership provided by

23

social scientists, economists, and organization theorists (Bennis 1989, Stogdill 1974, Barnard 1968).

The next section sets out the theoretical lay of the land and provides detailed descriptions of the relative value that specific personal attributes and positions hold for individuals eager to shepherd policy, both within the party hierarchies and within the committee system. These qualities are explored for both officeholders and aides.

The inventory of the actual leaders identified by the study participants as playing the commanding roles in one or more of the six policies under consideration form the basis of the empirical section entitled "Remapping the Leadership Terrain." Here, I test the extent to which a variety of personal attributes, institutional positions, and contextual conditions correspond with attaining leadership recognition in the House.

In identifying leaders first and foremost by their recognized abilities to attract votes in committee rooms and on the chamber floor and only secondarily by their formal positions and personal talents, we are in a position to analyze more precisely than heretofore the phenomenon of leadership and its correlates. In doing so, we minimize the risk of omitting leaders who come into prominence through unconventional means. Also, we are poised to compare personal talents such as substantive expertise and political savvy across an array of formal positions known to bear influence.

Personal Attributes, Positions, and the Lay of the Land

Personal Dimensions of Leadership

Only when congressional insiders develop a pronounced following, sufficiently large to be noticeable to people outside their immediate work environment, do they meet my criterion of leadership. Of all the personal attributes that would-be leaders may bring to their coalition work, the following seem particularly important: tenure, political ideology, electoral vulnerability, expertise, and interpersonal style.

Tenure
By rule and custom, the most senior members of the chamber ascend to positions of rank, elected positions of leadership for officeholders and appointed positions of authority for staff. Also, formal positions aside, it is often the most experienced veterans of the institution who command the attention of their more junior colleagues (Kingdon 1981). Battle-scarred policymakers remember the deals that worked and failed in past efforts to build support around particular issues. Such institutional memory, to say

nothing of the knowledge that comes with presiding over years of informational briefings and public hearings, makes the senior officials and aides attractive coalition builders.

Political Ideology

There are few disagreements about the meaning of political ideology. At the far left end of the ideological continuum are liberals who favor government interventions to solve social ills. At the far right end of the continuum are conservatives who prefer the remedies from the actions of free people, unencumbered by government regulation, however well intentioned. Where leaders reside along the ideological continuum is an open question. At times, the rank and file of each party look for leaders who will take extreme stands on the issues and stubbornly pursue them without compromise (Little and Patterson 1993). At other times, would-be followers disdain drastic measures and inflexible pronouncements. In such circumstances, the leaders with the most sizable followings are likely to be the ideological moderates, not the radicals from either party (Peabody 1976). We examine the political ideologies of the leaders who emerged to steer these six issues to discern if there is a favored temperament, ideologic extremist or moderate.

Electoral Vulnerability

House incumbents succeed in securing reelection at astonishing rates (better than 90 percent), oftentimes with very comfortable margins of victory (better than 20 percent). Still, according to Gary Jacobson (1992), the upsets come unannounced and with fearsome regularity. Indeed, political scientists find ample evidence to suggest that legislators operate under the constant threat of losing the next election (Fenno 1978, Mann 1978). The question before us is: Does electoral vulnerability play a role in officeholders' decisions to champion controversial issues? Arguably the sort of high-stakes, broad-scoped policies, the conditions that call for gutsy national leadership, are the most indefensible in terms of meeting the needs of voters back home. If this reasoning is accurate, those who promote the issues at hand may be more electorally secure than the followers who stay out of the limelight.

Expertise

Leaders need to know what it takes to make an ally out of an enemy and have the resources to do something about it. The process of conversion can take different forms. When leaders structure choices in such a way that the opposition is tricked or trapped into compliance—what William Riker (1986) calls "heresthetics"—they apply what I call *political expertise*. The changed behavior may have nothing whatsoever to do with the specifics of the policy. Rather, support is accrued through clever manipulation of agendas (what is admissible in committee and on the floor), the sequencing of votes, and the rhetorical dimensions on which the matter is discussed. While it is easiest to think of elected party leaders and committee kingpins (e.g., Jim Wright [D-Texas], Newt Gingrich [R-Georgia], and John Dingell [D-Michigan]) when we conjure up images of raw political expertise, the institution invites power wielders of this ilk at every level, even among staff (Light 1992, Bisnow 1990, Loomis 1979, Malbin 1980). And the aides who are particularly adept at preempting trouble through their clever use of the rules and insider knowledge of what it takes to transform adversaries into supporters may very well develop widespread reputations for political prowess.

Substantive expertise refers to the possession of subject-matter knowledge of an issue under consideration. This type of expertise is in high demand early in the life of a policy initiative, because at this juncture the legislative language is most fluid, and there remain a sizable number of undecided legislators who are on the lookout for terms they can support. To take advantage of the situation, issue leaders need the full command of their subject to envision alterations that bring new colleagues to the fold without risk of eroding the existing support. While officeholders and aides may be equally equipped to negotiate the fine points of the legislation, for many aides this expertise may be their only ticket to widespread recognition. Such is not the case for officeholders, who may inspire followers on a variety of grounds.

Interpersonal Style
The final two attributes—*affability* and *accessibility*—pertain to aspects of one's interpersonal style more than do either the substantive or the political expertise discussed thus far. In general, legislators are remarkably courteous, accommodating each other when it is in their power to do so. Consider as examples the committee assignment process (Ray 1982, Bullock 1976), the scheduling of floor votes (Oleszek 1988, B. Sinclair 1983), and the selection of witnesses for public hearings (DeGregorio 1993, Loomis 1988). Yet, as is evidenced when John Kasich's confrontational manner is contrasted with Martin Sabo's conciliatory management style, elected officials, regardless of their approach, can succeed if their style fits the challenge.

> The two men's thoroughly different styles are almost ideally suited to their diametrically opposite roles on the Budget Committee. The diligent, consensus-building [Martin O.] Sabo has the task of holding his

party's left and right wings together behind a Clinton budget proposal that makes neither extreme truly happy. The more flamboyant [John R.] Kasich, on the other hand, has set out to energize the hopelessly outnumbered Republicans in a campaign to create maximum chaos among Democrats while rehabilitating the GOP's reputation for thoughtful budgeting. By most accounts, both men have succeeded far beyond expectations. (Hager 1993a, 654)

This recent example, taken from the battle over the fiscal year 1994 budget resolution, depicts two adversaries whose styles fit the times. Also, for rank-and-file members who may prefer a more conciliatory approach from the leading Republican on the Budget Committee, there was no option. Formal leaders can monopolize the field, regardless of style, in a way that staff may not. Staff members are easily replaced. If for no other reason than their numbers, it is reasonable for legislators to root out abrasive staff and ally themselves to competent professionals who are both trusted and pleasant. If this conjecture is right, affability will be more important in selecting staff leaders than in selecting elected leaders.

Finally, I examine the leaders' accessibility to others. Veteran Hill watcher Christopher Matthews (1988) offers a prescription for leadership when he describes how "great politicians . . . forge alliances, make deals, manipulate enemies and bolster their reputations, all while building strong networks of alliances" (14). By way of contrast, it is timidity and isolation that characterize the unsuccessful pol. "Rather than recruit allies, they limit their horizons to missions they can accomplish alone. Instead of confronting or seducing their adversaries, they avoid them" (15).

Accessibility is important to leaders and followers alike. Leaders cannot afford to ignore potential followers who care about the pending policy, particularly when every new contact offers hope of discovering a creative, politically feasible solution. Furthermore, the representatives who are in search of competent leaders value some amount of direct access as well. First, individuals who have an interest in the policy will want to communicate their preferences to the individuals in charge. Moreover, the followers may have political or substantive insights that will help the leaders succeed in attaining the desired result.

The individuals who are identified as leaders by the study participants may attract the allegiance of House officeholders through substantially different means. For the reasons noted, I expect to find a correspondence between leadership recognition and several personal attributes. For officeholders, tenure, electoral vulnerability, and political ideology may make a difference between notice and obscurity in shepherding bills to passage. And several additional attributes may matter for both officeholders and staff who successfully assume leadership functions. These include political expertise, substantive expertise, accessibility, and affability. Because of their different stations in the institution, political expertise may correspond more with leading officeholders, and substantive expertise, affability, and accessibility may be more telling for staff.

Structural Dimensions of Leadership: Officeholders and Aides

Officeholders
In the House, two mechanisms vie for attention when it comes to building the support necessary to pass legislation: political parties and congressional committees. To the extent that party leaders approach their tasks aggressively with vision and talent, they have the potential to affect the fortunes of rank-and-file officeholders as well as the fates of countless controversial pieces of legislation. By using position in the party hierarchy as a criterion of leadership, we know to expect some formal party leaders to appear on the advocates' list of champions. Owing to the breadth of the legislative agenda and the complexity of the issues that come to a vote, we can also anticipate that these leaders will take a backseat to the substantive specialists who head up the congressional committees and subcommittees (Hall 1992, Kiewiet and McCubbins 1991, C. Evans 1991).

Table 2.1 lists (1) the number of positions that provide useful vantage points to persons seeking power, and (2) the number of people brought into the leadership fold with each successive layer of institutional structure. There are more positions (602) than there are officeholders (435) to fill the positions. Scholars attribute the explosion of subcommittees, caucuses, task forces, and the authority figures who spearhead each to the maturity and professionalism of the modern Congress. No longer the ragtag group of one- and two-term amateurs who characterized the early days of the republic, the House is made up of ambitious career politicians who want to retain their seats in the national legislature. To this end, they create for themselves myriad niches from which to gain credibility, positive media coverage, and credit as movers and shakers on Capitol Hill (Mayhew 1974). Furthermore, because incumbents rarely run in opposition to one another, it is safe for them to accommodate one another's needs for positions that accrue visibility and influence (Ray 1982, Westefield 1974).[2] In some ways, the growth in the whip system and other informational channels used by the two political parties is a response to the explosion of committees and, more important, to the decentralization of power that the committees foster in the institution (Little and Patterson 1993).

The top row in table 2.1 refers to the 18 individuals who hold positions within the Democratic and Republican party leadership. This tiny circle of leaders holds 3 percent of the existing command posts and represents 5 percent of all members who bear a title. There is remarkably little overlap here, furthermore, from one layer of structure to the next. Only one of the full standing committee chairs, of which there are 42 in all, simultaneously holds a post in either of the two party leadership offices. Out of the 264 available subcommittee leadership posts, only 41 go to individuals who already hold a title on the standing committees or in the party leadership. The balance of the positions, 213 in all, serve as bases of power for 172 new, as yet unranked officeholders. Although there is some duplication at this level, with members leading multiple subcommittees, these posts disperse opportunities for influencing policy to more representatives than any other structure in the institution. Subcommittee leadership posts account for 44 percent of the available positions and 53 percent of all members who bear a title.

Only with select committees, task forces, and informal caucuses do the leadership positions become secondary rather than primary avenues for influencing policy. As evidence of this, notice that only 38 persons brought into the leadership fold through informal congressional groups (ICGs) hold no other formal positions of authority. And although the ICGs represent 20 percent of the available positions, they comprise only 12 percent of the leadership pool. Finally, as decentralized as the House is,

TABLE 2.1.   Formal Positions Granting Opportunities for Leadership Involvement in the U.S. House of Representatives, 100th Congress

	Positions		People[a]	
	#	(%)	#	(%)
Party leadership posts	18	3	17	5
Standing committee chairs	42	7	41	13
Standing subcommittee chairs	264	44	172[b]	53
Select standing committee/				
task force chairs	48	8	18	6
Informal congressional groups	120	20	38	12
Party whips	110	18	36	11
Total	602	100	322	100

Note: Within the chamber, 113 individuals (26 percent) have no formal title of authority.

[a]Individuals are listed once for the most prestigious position that grants them an entrée in the leadership ranks. Secondary positions are not included in this count.

[b]The number of individuals who obtain a formal leadership rank at this layer of the structural hierarchy is as small as it is for two reasons. First, party leaders (8) and standing committee leaders (33) retain 41 positions for themselves. Second, rather than distributing the remaining 213 titles to different individuals, 172 officeholders share the balance.

the 602 titles are distributed to 322 members, leaving 113 of the 435 members with no formal title whatsoever. Moreover, as titles differ in the privileges they bestow, so too do individuals differ in their capacity for using the resources they have.

While particularly clever individuals may attract a following from an obscure station within the institution, there are notable differences among committees and standing within committees that benefit some members more than others. Taking committee designations first, at any one time the average representative holds seats on two standing committees and four subcommittees. Both types of panels play formidable roles in the legislative process. Whereas membership on a parent committee provides opportunities for blocking or promoting the gains made in the smaller work groups, the subcommittees do most of the early formulation and, recently, much of the follow-through (Dodd and Oppenheimer 1993b, Hall and Evans 1990). Because bills are often simultaneously referred to several committees, moreover, the representatives best poised to wield power will be those with jurisdictional legitimacy over two or more of the committees of referral.

Six committees are more powerful than any others. Rules, Appropriations, and Ways and Means head up everyone's list and have done so for decades because they have purview over important policy matters (i.e., taxing and spending), or they have procedural privileges over other committees (Smith and Deering 1990, Jewell and Chi-Hung 1974). The more recent powerhouses are Energy and Commerce, Armed Services, and Budget (Dodd and Oppenheimer 1993a, 1989a). Other committees appeal to members because their jurisdictions offer opportunities for correcting social ills (e.g., Judiciary and Education and Labor) and serving constituents (e.g., Agriculture, Interior and Insular Affairs, and Public Works) (Smith and Deering 1990, Fenno 1973).

Some members supplement the power that comes to them through their committee positions by joining one or more of the informal congressional caucuses. Like select committees, these groups have no authority to write laws. Nonetheless, they attract media attention, money, and staff, and with these resources their members assemble the data, the arguments, and the visibility from which to take the lead and gain a following (Shaiko 1991, Hammond 1990, Kornacki 1990, Loomis 1988).

When it comes to discerning the leaders within committees, the most logical place to start is with the elected positions: the committee chair and ranking minority leader. Whereas there may be informal pressures to accommodate one's colleagues of both parties on the committee, the chair has all the procedural advantages.[3] The chair decides which issues merit the national attention of a public hearing as well as who will testify and when (DeGregorio 1993, Krehbiel 1991). Even the subsequent and formidable decisions about when and how to debate the bill clearly favor the chairs (Smith and Deering 1990, Fiorina and Shepsle 1989, Bach and Smith 1988).

Congressional Staff

There are notable differences in the opportunities the institutional structure awards officeholders and aides. To begin, congressional staff members are constrained by the fact that they are not elected. Second, they serve from one and only one vantage point: a party leader's office, a committee post, or an individual member's office. Third, to some extent, staff power is derivative; it spills over from their bosses (Salisbury and Shepsle 1981). Still, the unelected bring varying amounts of vision and talent to the job, and I anticipate that some of them achieve recognition as leaders in their own right. I speculate that the breadth of their following depends largely on the position they hold in the institution.

Because every bill of any consequence is initially formulated in committee, staffers in these positions are well situated for developing a following on the issues within their panels' jurisdictions. From the foregoing discussion on committee appeal, furthermore, I expect that the officeholders and aides who are affiliated with Energy and Commerce or Appropriations will be recognized for leading a wider array of issues than individuals associated with narrowly circumscribed committees such as Agriculture, Education and Labor, or Judiciary.

Legislative assistants (LAs) who operate out of members' personal offices are likely to attract a varied collection of devotees not linked to a narrow stripe of issues. These aides are called upon to assess both the political and the substantive aspects of pending policies (Rundquist, Sneider, and Pauls 1992, Fox and Hammond 1977). And because they attend to a variety of legislative matters—depending on the interests of their bosses—they are in positions to become policy generalists. This is particularly true in the House, where officeholders have limited personal staff to devote to policy matters.

Staffers who work with the Speaker, majority leader, minority leader, or whips enter policy formulation during the final deliberative stages of the process. As a result, they can hardly be expected to fashion a coalition based on a clever repackaging of the substantive provisions. Rather, what heightens their opportunities for commanding a broad, nonissue-specific House following is their knowledge of procedure as well as their intimate familiarity with what it takes to woo undecided partisans, two skills that go hand in hand with their staff positions.

Different institutional positions offer different vantage points, and vantage points dictate who can legitimately intervene in a struggle for power and who is recognizable in their performance. Furthermore, no amount of opportunity and visibility will buy a bungler a following. Leaders need large stores of personal talent—ideas, skill, and commitment—to steer a controversial bill through to successful passage.

Propositions

As decentralized as power sharing is in the U.S. House of Representatives, not everyone is a leader. Common sense and informed judgment tell us that an accurate, and indeed more meaningful, count of congressional leaders is likely to number more than the 5 percent of members holding party posts (16 percent if whips are included in the count) and less than the 74 percent of all members bearing a title. Because followers are free to pick and choose the leaders with whom they want to ally themselves, leadership appeal is somewhat subjective.

When it comes to the personal side of power, I posit that the individuals who have seniority, electoral security, substantive know-how, political savvy, accessibility, and affability will have the easiest time eliciting the confidence from others that is required of a leader. Whether ideological moderates have an easier or more difficult time attracting the followership of rank-and-file House members is an open question.

I expect officeholders to prefer the leadership of officeholders to that of staff when the issues are of a political nature and, even more certainly, when the issues arouse public attention. The time when representatives are most likely to discount the leadership of staffers (the only House insiders not to have encountered the pressures of an election) is when the representatives believe their votes are being watched by interested constituents. By contrast, the policies that are inaccessible to untrained professionals give expert staff a leadership advantage over most officeholders (save perhaps the committee leaders themselves). In addition, I expect the two interpersonal attributes under investigation here—accessibility and affability—to be more important in the selection of staff leaders than elected leaders.

From the foregoing review of institutional positions, I predict that some posts are more advantageous than others. Officeholders have more privileges than aides. Committee leaders have more privileges than nonranking members. The Speaker and the majority leader are the only individuals with authority to direct bills to particular committees and schedule votes, respectively. In every case, members of the majority party have advantages that minority members lack. Counted among these perks, for example, are agenda-setting privileges and larger staffs (Hall 1993).

Congressional committees are unequal as well. Those with authority over taxing and spending and those with active and expansive agendas should offer the best platforms from which to lead. It stands to reason, furthermore, that substantive expertise should go hand in hand with committee position. And the individuals with the commitment and staff it takes to become fully apprised of an issue should be the committee leaders and their staff.

Remapping the Leadership Terrain

Leadership: The Personal Side of Power

The study participants find that the elected and the unelected serve as issue leaders for rank-and-file members of the House. Table 2.2 breaks down the observations along two dimensions. The row figures differentiate officeholders from aides. The column figures differentiate among qualitatively different types of leaders. Not surprisingly, a larger proportion of officeholders (252, or 58 percent of all officeholders) than aides (139, or 5 percent of all aides) are noticed for their ability to attract a following in the chamber. Of greater interest, perhaps, is the staffers' share of the leadership pool. The unelected policy experts represent nearly 36 percent of the entire cadre of House leaders.

Within the leadership group, there is a further breakdown into low-profile and high-profile leaders. This distinction rests on the level of recognition each leader engendered among the study participants. With 15 to 20 respondents reporting per issue, using the threshold of three or more citations as a measure of high-profile leadership status, at least 20 percent of the observers agree on the designation. Of the 117 individuals to achieve this threshold, 83 percent are officeholders.

Last, within the high-profile category there are specialists and generalists. This division speaks to the range of one's leadership appeal. The individuals who figure on one or two issues exclusively court a narrow, issue-specific following relative to the leaders whose names surface on three or more issues. The disparity between the recognition awarded officeholders and aides returns again, with elected officials constituting 97 percent of the generalist category and aides appearing almost imperceptibly.

Table 2.3 provides a thumbnail sketch of baseline leadership attributes. The modal House leader is Democratic, experienced, ideologically distant from the center of the chamber (officeholders), electorally safe (officeholders), and knowledgeable. The display also permits two comparisons: one between elected and unelected leaders and one between leading and nonleading officeholders.

Majority (Democratic) party affiliation, while prominent among the

TABLE 2.2. Leadership Recognition: Officeholders and Aides in the U.S. House of Representatives, 100th Congress (percentages in parentheses)

| | Total Population | Total Recognized | | Recognized Leaders | | | | | | | |
| | | | | Total Low Profile[a] | | Total High Profile | | Specialists[b] | | Generalists[c] | |
	N	N	%	N	%	N	%	N	%	N	%
Officeholders	434[d]	252	(64.5)	155	(56.6)	97	(83)	59	(72)	38	(97)
Aides	3,000[e]	139	(35.5)	119	(43.4)	20	(17)	19	(28)	1	(3)
Total	3,435	391	(100)	274	(100)	117	(100)	78	(100)	39	(100)

[a]One or two cites.

[b]Three or more cites on one or two issues.

[c]Three or more cites on three or more issues.

[d]Stewart McKinny (R-Connecticut) died in 1987. As a consequence, the subsequent analysis uses a base of 434 instead of 435.

[e]This figure includes 1,305 legislative assistants (Twenhafel 1992) and 1,695 committee aides. The total number of committee aides was derived by taking the full complement of personnel assigned to congressional committees, as reported in Vital Statistics 1988–89, and subtracting a small portion, 14 percent, which accounts for the workers primarily engaged in clerical work.

elected and the unelected alike, is significantly more pronounced among the aides identified as leaders. Whereas 73 percent of staff leaders represent the majority party view, only 65.1 percent of the officeholders do. More likely than not, the imbalances within both cohorts and the pronounced gap in prominence between staff from the two parties are a function of House rules and not a reflection of qualitative differences among the aides or the principals who hire them.

My interpretation of the evidence rests on the nature of party politics in Congress. At the time of the study, the Democrats comprised 59 percent of the chamber, yet they account for 65.1 percent of the identified issue leaders (elected).[4] This is not surprising given the imbalanced distribution of perks that redound to subcommittee and committee chairs and formal leaders of the majority party. Individuals on the lookout for competent champions may be well advised to place their legislative fortunes in the hands of colleagues who possess such institutional advantages.

Next, while every member of the House, regardless of party affiliation, receives the same allowance for staffing their offices, no such parity exists with congressional committee personnel. The majority party con-

TABLE 2.3. Personal Attributes of Unrecognized House Officeholders, as Compared with Recognized Officeholders and Aides, in the 100th Congress (in percentages)

Attributes	Unrecognized Officeholders ($N = 183$)	Recognized Officeholders ($N = 249$)	Recognized Aides ($N = 130$)
Party (Democrat)	51.7	65.1[#*]	73.0
Tenure in Congress	8.3	12.3[#]	8.1
Political moderate[a]	32.4	31.3	n.a.
Margin of victory (1986)	70.6	74.0[#]	n.a.
Expertise[b]			
substantive	n.a.	38.9	37.3
political	n.a.	31.8*	20.1
Interpersonal style[b]			
accessibility	n.a.	44.8	51.5
affability	n.a.	21.8	23.1

Sources: Interviews supplemented with secondary data from Ehrenhalt, Amrine, and Duncan, 1987, and Brownson, 1987.

Note on significance: * $p \leq .05$ (difference of means between recognized officeholders and aides); [#] $p \leq .05$ (difference of means between recognized officeholders and unrecognized officeholders).

[a]Using the Americans for Democratic Action (ADA) score as a standard of comparison, the extremists include all officeholders whose ADA score falls one or more standard deviations from the chamber mean (51.3). Moderates score within one standard deviation to the left or right of the chamber mean. There are no comparable staff data.

[b]The advocates assessed whether the appeal of the named leaders pertained to these attributes.

trols approximately two-thirds of that staff complement, and these are the policy experts most equipped to assist their bosses with shepherding bills. This imbalance in available personnel may be explanation enough for why majority-party aides dominate as they do. There are more Democratic staff to be recognized.

There may be an ideological impetus to the pattern as well. Perhaps conservative officials who eschew an expansive role for the federal government involve their aides in the business of building support for their objectives less than liberals do. Because it is easier to block legislative initiatives than to promote them, conservative leaders may be capable of foiling liberal initiatives with fewer staff resources. If this characterizes the Republican condition, one can see a reason other than numerical disadvantage that explains the diminished role of minority staff.

While this scenario makes sense in the abstract, I believe it ignores the special conditions of the 1980s. At this time, the House Republicans had a strong leader in the White House. As a consequence, they had good reason to use their staff resources aggressively in pursuit of the conservative agenda Ronald Reagan espoused.

That Democrats account for a slim majority (51.7 percent) of the unrecognized (nonleading) officeholders (table 2.3), furthermore, is evidence that the partiality shown elected majority partisans in the selection of policy champions is not as marked as one might expect.

This result is consistent with other observations about political parties in Congress. The diversity of tastes among the Democrats undermines the power of their numerical majority (B. Sinclair 1995, 1992b; Rohde 1991). Moreover, to pass legislation of any consequence, coalitions need to be forged across party lines, and many interested Republicans take up the charge.

In terms of congressional tenure, officeholders substantially outstrip aides in average years of service: 12.3 and 8.3, respectively. Close to 50 percent of legislators, in contrast with 30 percent of aides, have 11 or more years of House experience (data not shown). And a full one-third of staffers, as opposed to 11 percent of officeholders, have served less than five years (data not shown). The disparity in mean years of service for officeholders who do and do not achieve recognition by the study participants is also four years.

Next, fewer than one-third of all representatives fall within one standard deviation of the average (51.3) ideology score prepared by the Americans for Democratic Action (ADA). Because this finding holds regardless of one's leadership recognition, we can be confident that no special political temperament facilitates leadership one way or the other.

The evidence on incumbents' electoral fortunes echoes more similarity than dissimilarity as well. While there is a statistical difference between the legislators' margins of victory, with leaders (74.0 percent) faring somewhat better than nonleaders (70.6 percent), both groups win handily. This outcome is not surprising, given the high rate with which voters generally return incumbents to the House.

When it comes to the respondents' assessments of what they find appealing in the officeholders and staff they identify as leaders, some but not all of my expectations are borne out by the data. For example, the evidence affirms the proposition that political savvy is an appealing characteristic of leading officeholders more than leading staff members. By contrast, we must reject the notion that substantive expertise and staff are uniquely related. When it comes to inspiring confidence in their followers, officeholders do better, sometimes markedly better, than staff. What is more, regardless of whether or not one is elected, more leaders are singled out for their substantive than their political expertise. The sentiment for discounting political savvy is captured in the following quotation, which is quite typical of the advocates' viewpoint: "Political expertise is nice if you can get it, but really what's important is someone who knows the issue and is willing to work on the relevant committee" (interview, July 30, 1992). In the opinion of most onlookers, the champions of a policy must know the issue inside and out. Indeed, knowing the issue takes prominence over knowing how to maneuver individuals through political gamesmanship.

The respondents enlighten us as well on the relative appeal of two interpersonal attributes. As expected, a greater proportion of staff leaders than elected leaders are pursued for their accessible styles: 51.5 percent and 44.4 percent, respectively. The difference is not stable, however, and could be a chance occurrence. From the respondents' point of view, moreover, accessibility is an appealing attribute of both officeholders and aides. Also, whereas I expected affability and staff leadership to go hand and hand more than affability and member leadership, the difference is negligible. It is noteworthy, moreover, that only 20-some percent of the leaders, any leaders, are valued for their pleasant interpersonal styles.

Leadership: The Structural Side of Power

The next couple of tables examine the way leadership recognition corresponds with institutional position. Here the performance of officeholders and aides is taken up separately. Table 2.4 reinforces the theme that not all committees are equal. Table 2.5 examines levels of leadership recognition according to formal positions of power held (e.g., chairs and ranking minority members of various congressional work groups as well as official party leaders and whips). The first breakdown squares well with conventional wisdom and prior research on the relative attractiveness of different committee assignments.

I expected that a sizable share of leaders would come from the five powerful committees previously discussed—Appropriations, Armed Services, Energy and Commerce, Rules, and Ways and Means—and they do. There is an additional hierarchy of committee prestige that may be even more useful to our purpose because it scores the relative appeal of all standing committees in the House. By keeping track of members' requests for committee assignments at the outset of each new Congress, Charles Bullock and John Sprague (1972) provide an ingenious measure of committee appeal—the traffic patterns that incumbents create as they depart from undesirable committees and move toward more desirable ones.[5] The following ranking, which was constructed using data from the 95th to the 99th Congresses, places Ways and Means, Appropriations, and Rules at the top of a three-tier system. Next among the semiexclusive committees are, in order of preference, Energy and Commerce, Armed Services, Foreign Affairs, Banking, Judiciary, Public Works, Agriculture, and Education and Labor. Budget, Merchant Marine, Post Office, and Interior head up the final nonexclusive tier, with Government Operations, Small Business, Science, and Veterans Affairs coming in last. Notice that the five prestige committees discussed earlier place first in the Bullock and Sprague list, boosting the credibility of both conventional wisdom and the committee request methods of assessment.

Turning to table 2.4, we see that three of the six prestigious committees discussed earlier launch an above-average (median = 19) number of leaders. They are Appropriations, Energy and Commerce, and Ways and Means. Foreign Affairs, Government Operations, Judiciary, Agriculture, and Banking also perform better than average, an outcome at least partially explained by their involvement in the issues or their role in House politics.

To facilitate the analysis, the table orders the committees by referral activity. The committee (Energy and Commerce) that receives the most bills (four) produces a sizable number of leaders. Within the next two categories (three and two bills, respectively) three-fifths of the panels perform well. The proportion of committees spawning an above-average number of leaders diminishes as one reads down the rest of the list, suggesting a positive relationship between a committee's referral activity and the number of leaders it produces.

Now consider the percentages in the column labeled *High Profile*. Here we see that four panels do exceedingly well in terms of producing leaders who are repeatedly recognized by the study participants. Of particular interest is the Rules Committee. While the panel did not produce the numbers of champions of other larger panels, notice that more than 80 percent of its recognized members fit in the high-profile category. The respondents explained the way their approach to Rules was different from other committees. The following remark captures a sentiment that was repeated again and again: "The leadership and the people from the Rules Committee get involved towards the end" (interview, July 8, 1991). This and other respondents spoke about the party leadership and the Rules committee in one breath, as if they were one entity: "You go in and talk with the [substantive] committee people on a regular basis, the doors are

TABLE 2.4. Recognized Officeholders: Committee Assignments, Referral Activity, and Level of Recognition

Number of Studied Bills Referred to Named Committee	Officeholders Recognized[a]	Level of Recognition	
		Low Profile[b] (%)	High Profile[c] (%)
Four Bills			
Energy and Commerce	22	64	36
Three Bills			
Banking	25	72	28
Education and Labor	18	56	44
Foreign Affairs	28	61	39
Rules	10	20	80
Ways and Means	28	25	75
Two Bills			
Agriculture	38	55	45
Government Operations	20	70	30
Judiciary	20	65	35
Merchant Marines	114	71	29
Public Works	19	84	16
One Bill			
Armed Services	19	74	2
Interior	21	81	19
Science	20	85	15
Small Business	11	73	27
Veterans Affairs	10	70	30
No Formal Referral			
Appropriations	33	70	30
Budget	19	42	58
District of Columbia	6	67	33
House Administration	12	75	25
Post Office	9	89	11

Note: The source on committee assignments is Ehrenhalt, Amrine, and Duncan 1987.

[a]The 252 identified leaders hold multiple committee assignments, resulting in higher numbers of committee citations.

[b]One or two cites on one or two issues.

[c]Three or more cites on one or more issues.

always open. With [Speaker] Wright, [Minority Leader] Michel, [Majority Leader] Foley, and the Rules Committee people, you don't have the same sort of constant interchange" (interview, June 24, 1992). Many participants also expressed confidence that the Rules committee does the bidding of the majority-party leadership. As a consequence, they sometimes go to the party leaders and entirely sidestep members of Rules. Then too, there are many instances when neither contact is critical: "Our issues are not that close, so we typically don't go to the Rules Committee or the formal party leaders" (interview, July 7, 1992). On many issues where the floor vote is not anticipated to be close, it is considered foolhardy to request access with these individuals. Thus, different situations call for the assembly of different leaders, and it is the members of the Rules Committee, and, secondarily, the party leaders who are most readily dismissed.

Ways and Means offers no surprise in its capacity for generating legislative heavy hitters. Foreign Affairs performs better than expected, but the evidence is consistent with the international flavor that permeates these and other contemporary issues. According to the respondents, members of Foreign Affairs were poised and ready to play commanding roles with regard to legislation on the war on drugs, trading imbalances, nuclear testing, and the communist threat in Nicaragua. Similarly, the looming budget deficit provided the impetus for members of the Budget Committee to take the lead even when none of the issues were formally referred to them.

Next in the analysis we look for relationships between the four leadership designations and the possession of particular House titles, such as party leader, whip, and chair or ranking member on the various congressional panels.

The evidence in table 2.5 shows a strong link between those who are identified as leaders and those who hold duly elected positions of leadership within the institution. This interpretation comes from comparing the percentages in the four right-hand columns, which include ascending levels of leadership recognition. The relevant figure in the leftmost column details the total percentage of officeholders who reside in a particular position within the chamber. Take party leaders first. They represent a very exclusive group of officeholders, only 3.9 percent of the entire chamber. Yet these vantage points almost guarantee notice.[6] Only 1.7 percent of all House members who go unrecognized as issue leaders are from this pool. When noticed for their leadership prowess, party leaders are often observed promoting a broad cross section of issues, not ones narrowly circumscribed by a committee seat. The zero recognition in the specialist column attests to this interpretation.

House whips, some elected and some appointed, are the eyes and ears of the Democratic and Republic leadership. Together they constitute 23.9

percent of the chamber overall and 20.6 percent of those who are unrecognized as leaders. Unlike the party bosses, moreover, they achieve highest recognition (35.6 percent) as specialists, that is, for championing narrow policy areas.

What is important to our understanding of House leadership are the patterns evident in the table. The percentage of individuals who receive no leadership recognition whatsoever is in every row lower than the percentage of individuals in the group as a whole. The difference is most pronounced for subcommittee leaders, about a ten-point spread. Also, in every case, the percentage of recognized leaders is higher in the low-profile category than in the unrecognized category. Here again, the biggest jump is among the subcommittee group. Examining the difference between the two high-profile columns, the result is mixed. In only half of the rows (leaders of the parties, select committees and task forces, and caucuses) do the percentages continue to increase. In every instance, however, the figures in the high-profile, generalist column rise, sometimes markedly over the low-profile column. The overall pattern strongly supports the conclusion that leadership is inextricably linked to position.

When it comes to examining leadership recognition in terms of the four settings where policy-oriented staff typically work, we lack comparison figures on the whereabouts of all congressional aides (e.g., those identified as well as those not identified). We cannot determine with

TABLE 2.5. Levels of Leadership Recognition Broken Down by Formal Positions of Power Held by Officeholders within the U.S. House of Representatives (in percentages)

Position	Positions[a] Available as Platforms for Recognition	Leadership Recognition			
		None	Low Profile[b]	High Profile[c]	
				Specialist	Generalist
Party leader	3.9	1.7	3.2	0.0	23.7
Whip	23.9	20.6	23.4	35.6	23.7
Committee leader (Chair/Ranking Minority)					
standing committee	9.7	5.0	8.4	22.0	18.4
subcomittee	49.3	38.9	56.8	55.9	57.9
select committee and task force	9.5	3.9	11.0	10.2	28.9
caucus	21.5	17.2	21.9	28.8	28.9

$N = 432$.
[a]Column totals do not equal 100 percent because officeholders can serve in more than one capacity.
[b]One or two cites on one or two issues.
[c]Three or more cites on one or more issues.

confidence, therefore, if the relative difference between various committee platforms and leadership recognition is a meaningful one or simply a reflection of the institution's hiring practices. For example, even without precise information, we know that the parties' leadership staff represent a very small corps of professionals relative to committee and personal office staff. We know, further, that a larger share of committee staffers than personal office staffers are assigned to policy-oriented work (Rundquist, Sneider, and Pauls 1992, Twenhafel 1992, Fox and Hammond 1977).

Mindful of these tendencies, and even though a larger proportion of staff leaders come from standing committees than from anywhere else, we cannot confidently conclude that committees offer their employees better vantage points for attracting a following. Rather, it appears that the leadership recognition in the four work settings, as shown in table 2.6 by reading down the column labeled *Total,* roughly corresponds with overall House employment practices.

Elsewhere in the table, however, there are indications that some work settings are indeed better than others in terms of one's level of recognition. For example, the only group of aides to appear in the high-profile, generalist category are staffers from party leadership offices. Second, staff of both standing committees and subcommittees have a strong footing in the high-profile, specialist categories. And, controlling for their overall recognition, both of these groups do well relative to personal office staff. To see this, compare the groups' share of total recognition (40.7, 27.8 and 25.9 percent, respectively) with their share of specialist status (44.4, 27.8 and 11.1 percent, respectively). In each case, save among the personal office staff, the percentages hold steady or increase. This aspect of the analysis indicates that staff who work for a committee may have an easier time establishing a following than staffers who operate out of a representative's office.

TABLE 2.6.   Formal Positions Held by Recognized House Aides in the 100th Congress (in percentages)

Position	Total	Level of Recognition		
			High Profile[b]	
		Low Profile[a]	Specialist	Generalist
Party Leadership Office	5.6	2.2	16.7	100.0
Standing Committee	40.7	40.5	44.4	0.0
Subcommittee	27.8	28.1	27.8	0.0
Personal Office	25.9	29.2	11.1	0.0

$N = 108$.

[a]One or two cites on one or two issues.

[b]Three or more cites on one or more issues.

Leadership: The Implications of Partnership

Because of the fact that officeholders and aides hold qualitatively different positions in the chamber, we have, out of necessity, analyzed their accomplishments separately. Nonetheless, it is important to examine leadership recognition as it relates to one's position in the *staff-member partnership*. Far more aides (96.2 percent) are cited as being key players along with their bosses than are representatives cited along with one or more aides (33.1 percent). Furthermore, the difference is highly unlikely to have occurred by chance (probability < .000). This comparison lends support to the notion that the staff-member partnership is decidedly more important for an aide to become a leader than for an officeholder to do so. One passage in particular describes the interdependence and asymmetry between member and aide.

> The members are very busy. If the aides are interested, they can badger the member to get involved. They are really key, and it would be counterproductive to cut them out because you would alienate them. If, however, the member is not interested and staff pushes hard, they will be told pretty promptly to lay off. (Interview, May 30, 1991)

Members determine the parameters of their involvement in an issue and that of their staff. Officeholders who are unwilling to commit what it takes to be out ahead on an issue are apt to discourage their aides from becoming overly visible in the matter. This flow of command goes far toward explaining the rarity with which staff are cited as leaders without reference to their bosses.

Leadership: The Relevance of Political Context

By breaking the data down now along two dimensions of the policies under study—high and low subject-matter complexity and high and low public salience—we examine two final propositions about the leadership prominence of officeholders and aides and, indeed, among officeholders themselves.

Recall from table 1.1 in the preceding chapter that three of the six issues contain highly technical language. The debate over lowering the limit on nuclear tests from 10 to 1 kiloton, a provision of the Defense Authorization Act of 1988 (H.R. 4264), turned primarily on the technical feasibility of detecting low-level blasts and the safety and effectiveness of our nuclear stockpile, should less testing occur. By and large, this debate was led by members and staff of the two committees most skilled in these matters: Armed Services and Foreign Affairs. The debate over the Omnibus Trade and Competitiveness Act of 1988 (H.R. 4848) entailed complex provisions having to do with economics, intellectual property rights, and domestic and international trading practices. In this case, the substantive breadth and complexity of the bill ensured its referral to more than 10 congressional standing committees. This, in turn, gave legitimate entrée to a plethora of individuals capable of taking command over narrow and discrete sections of the initiative. The Agricultural Credit Act of 1988 (H.R. 3030) was about banking and finance more than about farming, and the subject matter severely challenged the leadership capabilities of the Agriculture Committee. Indeed, members on Agriculture willingly shared the lead with members and staff from Banking and Energy and Commerce because those were the only individuals who truly understood the technical provisions.

Next, according to the study participants, only two of the bills captured much media coverage and subsequent public attention. They are Assistance to Central America (H.J.R. 523) and the omnibus trade bill (H.R. 4848). The administration locked horns with House Democrats over both these matters. The controversies were intense, in part because the initiatives sought to curtail the power of the executive vis-à-vis the Congress and in part because they made good fodder for presidential campaign politics (Hiatt and Shapiro 1988, Wehr 1988). The negotiations over nuclear testing were obscure by comparison, probably owing to the technical complexity of the bill's provisions. The measures to reform the farm credit and welfare systems aroused interest only among affected audiences: farmers, ranchers, bankers, and insurers in the first case and service providers and recipients in the second case. And, while the antidrug bill dealt with a subject about which there was much public concern, its period of deliberation was too brief (approximately one month) to attract much notice.

Before examining the data, consider this speculation of events. I expect a higher proportion of staff leaders to emerge when issues contain technically complex subject matter than otherwise. Most policy-oriented staff are hired for their substantive expertise, so they should have an advantage over officeholders who win campaigns for a variety of reasons, often having nothing to do with their knowledge of the issues. Next, I expect a lower share of staff to emerge among the leadership pool when issues attract public attention. When voters show some interest in legislative initiatives, officeholders have good reason to get some positive visibility for themselves, not for their aides. Another pattern is feasible as well: this time consider the number and diversity of leaders overall and ignore whether they are elected. When issues are technically complex, the proportion of leaders receiving repeated recognition from different advocates (e.g., the high-profile leaders) should increase because there are fewer substantively competent leaders to choose from. In contrast, when policies arouse the interest of the media and the public at large, more disparate officeholders and their accompanying aides may have an interest in taking command. Thus, we would predict finding a higher proportion of low-profile leaders when issues are salient than when they are not.

The breakdown of data in table 2.7 reveals how the diffusion of leadership changes when the policies are grouped into low and high complexity and low and high salience. The baseline figures for the entire sample are included in the left-hand column. Contrary to expectations, the staff share of the leadership pool changes little when the issues are complex. Furthermore, their presence increases by as much as 12 percent in the circumstance (high salience) that our naive guess predicted they would diminish in force. The marked change that is picked up along the high-salience dimension in the low-profile category, which includes officeholders as well as aides, may partially explain the change among staff alone. As predicted, leadership is far more diffused when the issues are salient. In the advocates' search for leaders, they perceive a host of champions, with remarkably little overlap from one observer to the next. Indeed, when the public is not watching, 62.6 percent of the leaders appear in the low-profile category as compared with 91.2 percent when the public is watching. As the number of elected leaders swells to take part in building the coalition, so too does the number of staff.

The complexity of the issue invites greater opportunity for leadership as well. To the extent that complex policies span several committees' jurisdictions, as omnibus trade did, legislators will be equipped to take command of different portions of the bill in keeping with the specialized knowledge they receive in committee. Through the practice of multiple referral and the division of labor in the congressional committee system, officeholders do exactly what David Mayhew (1974) said they would:

TABLE 2.7. Leadership Designations by Selected Policy Dimensions in the U.S. House of Representatives, 100th Congress (in percentages)

Leadership Designations	All Policies ($N = 388$)	Technical Complexity		Public Salience	
		Low ($N = 223$)	High ($N = 165$)	Low ($N = 286$)	High ($N = 102$)
Aide[a]	35.0	35.4	36.4	33.6	45.2
Low-Profile[b]	70.1	64.1	78.2	62.6	91.2

$N = 388$.

[a]The proportion of officeholders comprises the balance of each of these row figures.

[b]The proportion of high-profile leaders comprises the balance of each of these row figures.

They distribute opportunity. While he was speaking narrowly about the opportunity for claiming credit with one's constituents to safeguard reelection, these findings reveal how these two mechanisms—multiple referral and congressional committees—diffuse opportunities for leadership, even when the issues are complex.

To this point, the analysis includes only tests of bivariate relationships (e.g., the correspondence between party affiliation and leadership recognition *or* the relationship between experience in office [tenure] and leadership recognition). Now I use multivariate analysis (ordinary least squares) to estimate the separate effects of a single variable while holding constant the effects of several other explanatory variables. By regressing the dependent variable, the frequency with which the officeholders[7] achieve leadership recognition, on the individual, structural, and contextual characteristics that I associate with attaining this special status, I arrive at some findings that cannot be secured through simpler methods: the substantive importance of a series of explanatory factors and the stability of the observed relationships.

The study participants do not mention the leadership capabilities of 191 officeholders, and the named legislators are identified as leaders by as many as 22 respondents. With this variation in leadership recognition, we can address two questions. What factors determine whether an individual is identified as a leader (LEADERSHIP RECOGNITION in the equation that follows)? And within the elite circle of leaders, what differentiates those with numerous citations from those with one or two (LEADERSHIP PROMINENCE)?

Because it is assumed that the explanatory variables have independent effects on leadership recognition that are additive, the relationships can be described in the form of an equation. Below, the first equation (EQ1) models the determinants of leadership recognition, using as the basis of analysis all officeholders in the House ($N = 435$). The results are useful in explaining why some members emerge within the ranks of leaders while others do not. The second equation (EQ2) focuses on the named leaders ($N = 249$) and estimates the extent to which the explanatory variables contribute to the level of recognition that officeholders achieve. These results help us understand what it takes to become prominent relative to other leaders.

EQ1: $\text{LEADERSHIP RECOGNITION}_i = A + B_1(\text{TENURE}_i) + B_2(\text{PARTY}_i) + B_3(\text{MODERATE}_i) + B_4(\text{SECURITY}_i) + B_5(\text{PARTY OFFICE}_i) + U_i$

EQ2: $\text{LEADERSHIP PROMINENCE}_i = A + B_1(\text{TENURE}_i) + B_2(\text{PARTY}_i) + B_3(\text{MODERATE}_i) + B_4(\text{TALENT}_i) + B_5(\text{PARTY OFFICE}_i) + B_6(\text{PRESTIGE}_i) + B_7(\text{VANTAGE}_i)$

$$+ B_8(\text{STAFF}_i) + B_9(\text{SCOPE}_i) + B_{10}(\text{COMPLEXITY}_i) + B_{11}(\text{SALIENCE}_i) + U_i$$

where:

A	= the intercept term;
TENURE_i	= total years in Congress of ith officeholder;
PARTY_i	= a dichotomous variable taking on a score of 1 if the ith officeholder is a Democrat and 0 otherwise;
MODERATE_i	= an interval measure of the distance between the political ideology of the ith officeholder (measured by the Americans for Democratic Action) and the mean ADA score for the entire chamber;
SECURITY_i	= percentage of votes won by the ith officeholder in the 1986 campaign;
TALENT_i	= the personal attribute index score of the ith officeholder;[8]
PARTY OFFICE_i	= a dichotomous variable taking on a score of 1 if the ith officeholder holds a formal party leadership post and 0 otherwise;
PRESTIGE_i	= a dichotomous variable taking on a 1 if the ith officeholder holds a ranking position on one of five prestige committees and 0 otherwise;
VANTAGE_i	= the number of relevant (e.g., referral authority over the six considered bills) committees and subcommittees held by the ith officeholder;
SCOPE_i	= a dichotomous variable taking on a score of 1 if the ith officeholder achieved leadership recognition for championing a policy broad in scope and 0 otherwise;
COMPLEXITY_i	= a dichotomous variable taking on a score of 1 if the ith officeholder achieved leadership recognition for championing a technically complex policy and 0 otherwise;
SALIENCE_i	= a dichotomous variable taking on a score of 1 if the ith officeholder achieved leadership recognition for championing high-salience policies and 0 otherwise;
STAFF_i	= a dichotomous variable taking on a score of 1 if the ith officeholder employed staff who were themselves recognized as leaders; and
U_i	= the disturbance term.

By incorporating data available in the public record with the study participants' opinions about who is and who is not a leader, the first model estimates the effects of a number of attributes that theoretically contribute to one's leadership appeal. We have reasoned, for example, that office-holders who are experienced (TENURE), politically moderate (MODER-ATE), in the party of the majority (PARTY), assigned to a powerful committee (PRESTIGE), or in a party leadership post (PARTY OFFICE) are well-positioned to be seen and appreciated for their leadership skills in shepherding major policy. Because spearheading controversial issues is not without electoral risk, it also makes sense that those who accept the leadership challenge are more electorally secure (SECURITY) than those who decline.

The multivariate analysis reported in table 2.8 confirms some of these hunches but not all of them. LEADERSHIP RECOGNITION (EQ 1) corresponds positively with TENURE. What is more, the estimated effect (OLS column) of .10 can be sizable when one considers the range of years that House members serve (49 years). Two additional variables that are statistically stable and show modest effects are PARTY and VANTAGE. When it comes to being identified as a leader or not, there is a perceptible

TABLE 2.8.   Differentiating Leaders from Nonleaders

	All Officeholders	
	OLS	SE
Individual Attributes		
TENURE	.10	.00**
PARTY	.67	.29
MODERATE	−.01	.01
SECURITY	.01	.01
Position		
PARTY OFFICE	5.05	.74**
PRESTIGE	.14	.28
VANTAGE	.48	.09**
Constant	−.98	.78
Adjusted R^2	.21	
Significance F	.00	

Note: Valid $N = 434$. The table reports the unstandardized ordinary least squares (OLS) estimates and the standard errors (SE) of each estimate. If the null hypothesis that the parameter is zero were true, the probabilities (p) with which this outcome could have occurred by chance are as follows: ** $p \leq .001$, * $p \leq .05$. Logit analysis of the same model (with the exception that the dependent variable is dichotomized into two groups—those with and those without recognition) produces the same results. The OLS estimates are reported here because their interpretation is more straightforward.

advantage to being a member of the majority party. Also, the number of committees one sits on that have referral power over bills (VANTAGE) corresponds positively with LEADERSHIP RECOGNITION. This effect can be sizable as well when one considers the range of the variable (eight). The single best position for advancing officials into the leadership elite, however, is a position in the party hierarchy (PARTY OFFICE). This effect is large and stable. When other factors are controlled for, electoral vulnerability and political ideology do not count for much in becoming a leader in the House. Even holding a seat on a prestigious committee is unimportant when taken into consideration with other factors. Overall, these variables explain 21 percent of the observed variation in leadership recognition, leaving most of the variation unaccounted for.

The second model (table 2.9) includes the composite measure of an officeholder's substantive and political expertise (TALENT), a measure of staff involvement (STAFF), and the nature of the issues on which different individuals took up the lead (COMPLEXITY, SCOPE, and SALIENCE). This model explains 42 percent of the observed variation in leadership. And the estimated effects of several factors are stable ($p < .05$) and sub-

TABLE 2.9.   Explaining Levels of Recognition among Leading Officeholders

| | Leading Officeholders | |
	OLS	SE
Individual Attributes		
TENURE	.05	.02*
PARTY	.30	.37
MODERATE	−.01	.01
TALENT	.45	.22*
Position		
PARTY OFFICE	3.95	.78**
PRESTIGE	−.10	.34
VANTAGE	.35	.11**
STAFF	2.76	.37**
Policy		
COMPLEXITY	1.40	.39**
SCOPE	.58	.39
SALIENCE	.81	.37*
Constant	−2.14	1.08*
Adjusted R^2	.45	
Significance F	.00	

Note: Valid $N = 243$. The table reports the unstandardized ordinary least squares (OLS) estimates and the standard errors (SE) of each estimate. If the null hypothesis that the parameter is zero were true, the probabilities (p) with which this outcome could have occurred by chance are as follows: ** $p \leq .001$, * $p \leq .05$

stantively meaningful. TENURE, PARTY OFFICE, and VANTAGE continue to affect leadership as before. Also, no real change occurs in the lack of effects found in MODERATE and PRESTIGE. Once personal attributes and the nature of the issues are accounted for, however, party label loses its significance. (I return subsequently to this important discrepancy between the two models.) Of the two new variables that are included in this equation, STAFF substantially affects LEADERSHIP PROMINENCE (EQ 2), and its effects are stable ($p < .01$). Also, as expected, TALENT has an appreciable effect on LEADERSHIP PROMINENCE.

I interpret the differences in the effects of PARTY from one model to the next as follows. When there is little other information to go on, party identification, party office, and tenure are good criteria for singling out the leaders from the nonleaders. However, when discriminating among leaders and more is known about the players and the policies, party labels become unimportant. What supporters look for are experience, skills, and position.

When it comes to individual skills (TALENT), furthermore, there are two findings of note. According to the study participants, followers look for leaders who know both the subject matter *and* the politics of the issues they promote. The fact that these two concepts are analytically inseparable (endnote 8) challenges claims that a distinction is possible, that individuals specialize in one or the other of these talents but not both of them. Second, individuals' command of these skills tangibly boosts their prominence as leaders in the House.[9]

There are a number of ways to interpret the positive effect of STAFF on LEADERSHIP PROMINENCE. When lawmakers share the responsibilities for steering major policy with highly competent staff, the officeholders increase the likelihood that they (themselves) will be recognized as leaders. If for no other reason, staff expand the visibility of their bosses by freeing them to work with more people. As their contacts widen, the officeholders' prominence becomes more widespread. Also, STAFF may be capturing something not measured directly in this study. The lawmakers who share the shepherding of policy with their most competent staff may be the officeholders with the most commitment to act on an initiative. Thus, STAFF could be a reflection of commitment, something the advocates agree is a precondition of leadership (as will be discussed in chapter 5).

As suspected, the complexity of the issues and their salience to the public heighten the prominence of particular policy champions. In the first case, the same names may recur because these are the individuals with the expertise needed to foster arcane subject matter. In the second case, public attention in the media may contribute to the frequency with which certain individuals are relied upon. Even the lack of connection between SCOPE and this measure of leadership makes sense. If the dependent variable measured the number of leaders who shared in the process of promoting a cause instead of the frequency with which certain individuals are recognized as leaders, the result might be different. It will necessitate keeping track of the leadership networks that emerge over many more bills before this hunch can be tested.

These multivariate tests eliminate from serious consideration one factor (electoral security) that corresponded with leadership in the bivariate analysis (table 2.3), and they raise an important subtlety about a second ingredient, party affiliation, that evokes a conditional effect. Once other factors, such as tenure and position, are controlled for, one's margin of victory does not perform well in predicting leadership. And party labels, while useful in differentiating leaders from nonleaders, are not helpful in differentiating the most prominent from the least prominent leaders.

Other relationships that surfaced in the bivariate tests hold up well through the multivariate analyses. For example, consider the preliminary breakdowns between committee assignments and referral activity in table 2.4 and between leadership designations and the dimensions of the policies in table 2.7.

Summary and Conclusions

Where does this leave us? The individuals looked to for steering policy are more numerous and varied than may have been supposed. What is more, the burden of coalition building is shared among officeholders and staff, in a ratio of about two-thirds officeholders to one-third staff. This level of staff presence is stable, moreover, across policies that vary considerably in subject-matter complexity and public salience.

In keeping with voluminous research on the subject, the evidence on officeholders reaffirms the fact that the party hierarchies and the congressional committees spawn most of the named leaders. Still, several new subtleties come to the fore. First, while majority party status helps with initial recognition, it has no bearing thereafter. Other attributes pertaining to individuals' committee seats and personal talents are better indices of prominence within the leadership pool than is party label alone. Second, prestige committees launch fewer issue leaders than workhorse committees with active agendas and broad jurisdictions. The insight recommends that we pay closer attention to the *combination* of seat assignments any member holds, rather than any one position with admitted stature. Third, while a naive guess might suggest that leaders command the attention of their followers through *either* subject matter expertise *or* political expertise, these data support no such distinction. Instead, most issue leaders possess both attributes at once.

Next, differences between the leadership roles of the officeholders and aides come to light when the entire leadership pool is subdivided along two substantively interesting dimensions that emerged from empirical observation: the breadth of the leader's recognition by independent eyewitnesses and the breadth of the leader's involvement over disparate policy engagements. In the first breakdown, 82 percent of the high-profile leaders are officeholders, and the balance (18 percent) are aides. This finding suggests that staff leaders have a narrower band of followers than officeholders and, as a result, sometimes escape the notice of onlookers. In the second breakdown, officeholders completely dominate staff. Indeed, only one aide, who worked out of a party leadership office, was observed to have a commanding role in three or more of the six policies under investigation. This finding suggests that staff members are profoundly more limited than officeholders in the variety of issues they have the opportunity to lead. Even officeholders are limited in the extent to which they can range freely over far-flung policy concerns. The evidence for this conclusion comes from the fact that the generalists—the identified champions of three or more initiatives—operate largely from party leadership offices and ranking positions of top-tier committees.

There are both similarities and differences when we compare the criteria used to select officeholders and those used for aides. First, the members' leadership is primarily based in one of two places: their committee affiliations or a position in the party leadership. While committee positions serve as a dominant power base for the aides as well, a sizable proportion (25.7 percent) of the unelected leaders operate out of members' personal offices. It is important to note, moreover, that while they bring independent skills and energy to the struggle, staff leaders are almost always pursued in conjunction with the powerful officeholders who employ them.

When it comes to the interpersonal attributes of being accessible or affable, there are more similarities than differences between legislators and staff members. The leaders' appeal, regardless of their elected status, turns more heavily on their accessibility than their affability. What matters most, according to the respondents, is the leaders' political and substantive expertise. In each case, moreover, the officeholders' leadership appeal adheres to these qualities more than does that of the aides.

CHAPTER 3

The Advocates

Congress shall make no law abridging the freedom of speech or of the press; or the right of the people peaceably to assemble and to petition the Government for redress of grievances.
                    —First Amendment of the U.S. Constitution

There are winners and losers in almost every controversial measure that Congress adopts. To minimize their losses, advocates of myriad organizations pursue close working relationships with the legislators and staff who are most equipped to steer policy outcomes in line with the advocates' organizational interests. And the cumbersome structure of Congress, with its two chambers and numerous committees, slows down the policy-making process, giving ample opportunity for evaluation, promotion, and compromise along the way. Still, experience tells us that not all groups take similar advantage of their right to protest, as safeguarded for us in the U.S. Constitution.

Acknowledging that it is nearly impossible to observe and explain influence at work, this study does the next best thing. I examine two phenomena that are both observable in and fundamental to the exercise of power: political participation and access. In the belief that to have any influence whatsoever in the political process, one must be a player, I focus in this chapter on the determinants of political participation. Then in the next chapter, accepting John T. Tierney's (1992) insight that "access begets influence, and unequal access begets unequal influence" (204), I probe for disparities in the advocates' personal and organizational assets that may give rise to disparities in their access to Capitol Hill.

To illustrate what is common to many policy skirmishes that occur on Capitol Hill, I analyze three of the issues from the perspectives of the advocates who stood to gain or lose from the proposed legislation. The narrative follows an overview of the chapter.

Overview

Study of political participation on the part of organized groups has a long and rich history. In the section entitled "The Theory and Practice of Political Participation," I first review what we know about the formation and maintenance of privately organized groups,[1] drawing most heavily on the rational choice perspective first applied to interest groups by economist Mancur Olson (1965). Although there are competing theories that explain the political advocacy of groups, this approach offers the most satisfying explanation of behavior in settings as diverse as multimillion-dollar corporations and voluntary, citizen-led associations. There are three conceptually distinct ingredients to consider, each of which has a bearing on the group's emergence, activism, and subsequent survival: individual choice, institutional patronage, and political leadership.

The ingredients of individual choice and political leadership also go far toward explaining advocacy within the public sector. Certainly, state and local governmental entities encounter many of the same challenges that geographically dispersed, private-sector groups face when they attempt to mobilize members and navigate their positions through the halls of Congress. Also, timely information from allies in Congress advantages presidents and their administrative surrogates who must outwit legislative opponents to realize controversial presidential initiatives. What is distinctive and deserving of special elaboration is the advocacy that occurs on behalf of the president and the executive branch of government. Here the constitutional provisions for checks and balances and separation of powers create as many assets as they do liabilities for presidential aides when they attempt to lobby Congress. These and other institutional features of the Washington-based federal bureaucracy necessitate a brief primer on executive-legislative relations.

Theories about organized interests and bureaucratic politics leave us with two main impressions. First, organizations with ample stores of money, staff, and members (typically the for-profit and nonprofit occupational groups) overshadow the resource-poor participants (typically the cause-oriented, citizen-based groups). Second, there is a direction to the activity of mobilized interests. The parties who anticipate being harmed by policies that alter status quo arrangements with which they are comfortable are more likely to voice their concerns than parties who envision gaining from a legislative initiative.

The first of these impressions, in particular, is not well substantiated because the two methodological approaches that scholars use to study the behavior of organized interests—large-scale surveys and case studies—are incapable of getting at the truth. Large-scale surveys, which are well suited for describing the characteristics of the participating organizations and the tactics they employ to press these causes, are ill suited to examine the dynamics that are introduced by qualitatively different political battles. Case studies of the way organizations mobilize around singular policy confrontations offer rich detail about unique events. Using either method, in the end we are left wondering: What do these groups and others like them do under different circumstances?

The section entitled "Profiles in Action: The Evidence on Participation" addresses two questions that enlighten us on this mystery about political participation under changing conditions: (1) Does the makeup of the pressure community that emerged over six qualitatively different issues reveal a preponderance of for-profit and nonprofit organizations, as we would expect? and (2) Does the relative involvement of different types of groups vary when we control for differences in the political contexts of the issues (e.g., levels of public salience) and their subject matter (e.g., levels of complexity)?

Next, because it is often through coordinated action that groups assemble the information and contacts they need to acquire access to influential political leaders, no discourse of advocacy is complete without understanding the inducements and impediments to collaborative work among professional advocates. The second substantive section of this chapter presents the theory and the empirical evidence on two interrelated ways in which groups work with other groups: in *issue niches* and *in coalitions*. The first, "issue niches," is the compartmentalization of the pressure community into discrete and narrow policy subsystems. Groups specialize to conserve their resources and build reputations for themselves as recognized policy experts. As a consequence of their narrow issue foci, the vast majority of groups never encounter one another on the same political stage. I test the extent to which participants exhibit this sort of parallel political participation by breaking the sample down into six separate policy domains. Finding that groups restrict their attention to one of the six policies is consistent with the theory on issue niching.

Organizations' proclivities to conserve resources and develop specialized expertise also induce groups that reside within the same policy domain (or issue niche) to share information and coordinate their strategies. The ad hoc coalitions that result, while a common occurrence in the advocacy community, are scarcer in some policy domains than in others. We therefore observe the extent to which coalition activity corresponds with distinguishing features of the policies, their scope of application, subject matter, and contexts.

Throughout this review it is important to keep in mind one feature that is common to all the advocates, regardless of their base of operations.

Not having been elected to the House themselves, they are outsiders. They lack the legitimacy to engage in the negotiations that take place during two crucial phases of lawmaking—markups in committee rooms and debates on the chamber floor. To protect their interests, the advocates instead compete for the attention of the most influential legislators and staff who will espouse their positions and further their goals just as if the advocates were present to speak up for themselves. In the end, this is what political advocacy is all about.

The Cases and the Controversies

A cursory look at the substantive provisions and the anticipated winners and losers of a subset of the bills before us illustrates what is common to them all: major legislation is not neutral. It threatens some segments within society while comforting others, and in every case, professional advocates, speaking on behalf of a great many organizations, support and oppose the pending initiatives. All these organizations, through their advocates, try to pull the outcomes closer to their own visions of good public policy. Three examples follow.

The first example, the Agricultural Credit Act of 1987, had two main provisions: the bailout and the restructuring of the failing Farm Credit System (FCS). The bailout provision was intended to give family farmers more time to pay off their debts and reestablish their businesses, and the administrative restructuring was intended to stem the alarming rate of foreclosures that had nearly decimated the family-farm industry.

The bailout portion of the bill was lauded by farmers, ranchers, and their representatives. Commercial banks and insurance companies liked the bill because, for the first time, they would be permitted to move into this market. The Reagan administration supported change but wanted to minimize the costs to the taxpayer. To guard against giving too much to the powerful agriculture lobbies, the top executives at the Farm Credit System called in officials from the Treasury Department.[2] Still watchful of their own turf, however, were advocates from both the Farm Credit System and the Farmers Home Loan Bank System. The victims of this policy were some ailing farm credit system banks in the heartland of the country that would be eliminated in the plans to consolidate management.[3]

The passage of the Family Support Act of 1988, the second example, represented a legislative milestone for the 100th Congress. For the first time in over a decade, the lawmakers agreed on a way to attack the crippling cycle of poverty that ensnared 20 percent of American children (Rich 1988). The bill represented a marked departure from old welfare policies in that it was openly intended to get recipients of Aid to Families with

Dependent Children (AFDC) off welfare and back to work (*Washington Post* editorial, December 10, 1987). This feat would be accomplished, it was hoped, through a mixture of mandatory work requirements (exempting only mothers of children under three years of age), subsidized child care, job training, and financial aid (Rich 1987). To ease the transition from welfare dependency, the legislation would also provide transitionary health and welfare benefits. To lessen the costs to taxpayers, it would help single mothers track down delinquent fathers who had reneged on paying child support. And, for the first time, poor, intact, and functioning families—the so-called deserving poor—could count on some temporary government aid. The losers included (1) single mothers who preferred to stay at home with their children and not work, (2) fathers who had up to that point escaped their financial responsibilities, and (3) conservative American taxpayers who objected to any expansion of the welfare rolls as a wrongheaded solution to the problem of poverty.

The interest community that developed around this issue consisted of governors, state human service commissioners, welfare recipients, local government officials, and service providers. Even fathers had a spokesperson in the National Welfare Rights Reform Union, although of all the organized interests, they were probably the least visibly represented.[4] Advocates for the administration came from the White House (policy advisers), the Office of Management and Budget, and the Departments of Agriculture, Labor, and Health and Human Services. In every case, these advocates promoted the interests they were organized to advance and protect.

The final example is the Anti–Drug Abuse Act of 1988. Republican House members, especially eager to capitalize on the drug issue in their upcoming campaigns and backed by an active administration, fought for an extremely tough bill (Kenworthy 1988). The provisions included invigorating interdiction, ratcheting up the penalties for all drug offenses, and formally declaring a "war on drugs," using the administrative apparatus to call attention to the problem and appointing a first-ever "drug czar." Even in this legislative battle there were winners and losers. The two most controversial measures were (1) a mandatory death penalty for all criminals convicted of killing someone during a drug-related crime, and (2) drug screening of all federal employees.

While most citizens apparently stood to gain from the assurances of attaining a society freer of drugs, civil liberties groups and federal employees' unions fought what they perceived to be the erosion of personal rights to life and privacy. Many other groups, however, organized to support the get-tough measures aimed at prevention as well as the educational and counseling services aimed at rehabilitation. These groups were associa-

tions representing city mayors, law enforcement officials, professional service providers, and others who stood to gain from the statutory changes.
Citizen-based, cause-oriented groups such as Mothers Against Drunk Driving (MADD) made their support known as well. Working on behalf of the
president and his administration were advocates from the White House,
the Law Enforcement Assistance Agency, the Department of Health and
Human Services, and the Coast Guard.

These three vignettes highlight two main characteristics of political
advocacy in America. First, important policy changes of any consequence
always attract the attention of existing groups that are poised and ready to
press their cases on the decision makers. Second, multipronged policies
rarely receive simple positive or negative assessments from the interested
onlookers. Let me develop these points more generally.

The inventory of established groups organized and ready to influence
government policies and actions varies with one's selection base. For
example, many indexers and analysts count as advocacy groups only those
that have offices in the nation's capital. By such accounts the number of
groups in the late 1980s figured in the tens of thousands (Close, Bologna,
and McCormick 1989, Schlozman and Tierney 1986, and Salisbury 1984).[5]
But the Washington-based figure, while indicating the magnitude and
diversity of voices in the interest-group community, omits from consideration all organizations that launch advocacy campaigns from offices based
elsewhere around the country and agents from government who represent
the interests of the president, state governors, mayors, and the like. The
size of the pressure-group community that participated in the six bills
under study is markedly increased when we include for consideration the
private groups based outside of Washington (9.4 percent) and public
groups at all levels of government (37.5 percent).

The second aspect of political advocacy, that national policies of any
consequence rarely receive simple positive or negative assessments from
advocates, is, I contend, a product of the complexity and scope of governmental engineering. Supporters and foes alike typically find flaws that they
want corrected before passage. So it was with the Agricultural Credit Act.
Farmer cooperatives were on the brink of collapse, and they wanted government financing to help them out. Yet at the same time, they did not
want to lose autonomy in the upcoming restructuring. Nor was welfare
reform a cut-and-dried issue. Everyone wanted *something* to pass, but
there were major disagreements over the balance between supportive
inducements (the carrots such as job training and child care) and harsh
requirements (the sticks such as forced labor) (Rich 1987). The reception
of the antidrug bill was mixed as well. The most common complaint
among supporters was they wanted more—more funding for interdiction,

prevention, and rehabilitation. Furthermore, those who opposed the bill because it infringed on human rights had no quarrel with the remaining provisions (Kenworthy 1988). In all six policies, only 25 percent of the study participants reported taking clear stands in support of or in opposition to the stated policies. The vast majority of advocates gave the bills mixed reviews. They got involved to strengthen some provisions and to sabotage others within the same legislation.

The Theory and Practice of Political Participation

Advocacy from the Private Sector

The Theoretical Importance of Individual Choice
The foremost theorists on interest-group behavior concur that citizens participate in politics when it serves their interests to do so (inter alia Moe 1980, Berry 1977, Wilson 1973, Salisbury 1969, Olson 1965). Because the "something" is more likely to be a tangible good (such as discount travel fares and group insurance rates) than an elusive policy goal, it takes money and entrepreneurial talent to build and sustain an advocacy group. The groups that succeed beyond the difficult formative period do so, in part, because they receive assistance from external patrons who blandish them with money and valuable political information. Where private philanthropists may help a fledgling association overcome its early travails, political leaders offer the group's organizers valuable information on pending issues and upcoming votes. These tips from individuals in the know serve to sustain and strengthen groups. The groups gain credibility and stature as they are seen on the winning side of successive policy battles. Over time their success attracts members and patronage and leads to future success.

So from the simple notion that individuals' decisions to join (or not to join) a group rest on something other than personal commitment to the issue, we arrive at an elaborate explanation of group formation that entails entrepreneurial organizers and outside patrons—neither of whom would be essential if citizens just joined groups for the sake of joining. Furthermore, it is this construction of political participation that helps explain the numerical preponderance of some groups, such as occupational associations, and the relative scarcity of others, such as cause-oriented, citizen-based organizations (J. Walker 1991, Scholzman and Tierney 1986).

Academics, not wholly satisfied with the circular reasoning of the argument that individuals join groups because it pleases them to do so, have continued to refine the story. John Mark Hansen (1985), for example, observed that organizations are quicker to assemble around halting unwanted government intervention than around promoting government service. Thus, he profitably distinguished between governmental policies that incur a collective harm and those that promise a collective good.[6] At least two phenomena are at work here. Because it is far easier to defeat than to pass a bill in Congress, organizations that engage in blocking tactics can be fairly confident they will succeed. Also, when government threatens an existing market, the occupational community already exists to defend its turf. The group pays a marginal cost in a targeted advocacy campaign in exchange for a near-certain victory—diluting, if not stopping completely, the offending legislation.

Taking a slightly different tack, Robert Salisbury (1969) developed an exchange theory of interest-group politics. He links group emergence and early stability not so much with the bundle of incentives it takes to keep members happy as with the incentives it takes to engage group organizers through the formative years of the enterprise. He likens the interest-group leader—or "entrepreneur," in his terms—to the founder of a business. Both are willing to invest in the heavy start-up costs of their endeavors because they see sufficient personal rewards at the other end. While the business executive may see profit and a stable job, the interest-group leader, now executive director or Washington lobbyist, sees recognition and a stable job. The exchange theory of interest-group politics goes further than most in addressing the knotty question of group formation.

*The Theoretical Importance of Public and
Private Patronage*
Where Robert Salisbury (1969) explained group formation in terms of exchange theory, Jack Walker (1991) explains the growth and diversity within the interest-group community in terms of patronage. Both insights offer major contributions to the field. Here again our interest is in observing systematic biases that may account for the particular array of groups that survive and flourish within the advocacy community. Would-be interest-group leaders need funds to keep them and their organizations alive until such time as their mission, credibility, and accomplishments replenish financial resources on a secure and continuing basis. In Walker's (1991) view, there are two important ingredients to group formation and maintenance—clever organizers and, even more important, wealthy patrons. He contends that "group leaders learned how to cope with public goods dilemma not by inducing large numbers of new members to join their groups through the manipulation of selective benefits, but by locating important new sources of funds outside their immediate membership (77). Organization building is costly, and, according to this view, groups would not survive the expensive start-up phase were it not for the financial assistance of wealthy, committed sponsors.

If all groups need patrons to supplement their income from members, citizen-based groups are arguably the most needy of all. Citizen-based groups, or cause-oriented groups, as they are also called, have the fewest internal resources upon which to draw. They are disadvantaged relative to occupational groups because they have no focal point other than their mission. They may attract wealthy members, but they compete with kindred organizations for every dues-paying member they get. Contrast this with labor unions and trade and professional associations that have economic interests in common. They establish mechanisms for communication and coordination in the normal course of doing business. At little additional cost, these same networks can be used for promotional, political purposes. When cause-oriented groups organize, they start from scratch, unable to take advantage of a preexisting infrastructure (J. Walker 1983).

In light of these disparities, it is not surprising that King and Walker (1991) uncovered a pattern of external patronage that corresponds remarkably well with organizational need. Eighty-nine percent of citizen-based groups report being the beneficiaries of patronage. This figure is nearly 30 percent higher than the nonprofit's 60 percent rate and almost three times the level reported by for-profit organizations. What accounts for the favoritism shown citizen groups (their marketing, appealing causes, or both), we do not know. The trend in patronage, while probably not substantial enough to compensate for the other factors that systematically advantage occupational groups, nonetheless provides an important counterweight.

The Theoretical Importance of Political Leadership

As a political system, democracy places a premium on citizen involvement—if not in selecting its officeholders (electoral politics), then in guiding officeholders' decisions about what constitutes good public policy (governmental politics).[7] And changes in the media and Congress over the last thirty years (e.g., 24-hour news coverage, satellite images in real time, electronic voting machines on the House floor, and "government in sunshine" reforms) have intensified officials' dependence on public support. Lawmakers, for example, can not easily conduct secretive, behind-the-scenes negotiations and register voice votes. Now nearly every official action of a House member is captured on television or in the written *Congressional Record.* While we can all applaud these changes for their positive effects on legislative accountability, they have a negative side as well. Formerly, a dozen or so senior members—usually the party leaders and a few relevant committee chairs—could quietly and quickly gain the support of other lawmakers. Now the champions of big national initiatives must educate the mass public in hopes that citizens will convince their representatives to go along with what the leaders want.

To be effective partners in the policy-making process, citizens need to understand when and how they fit in. As Steven J. Rosenstone and John Mark Hansen (1993) point out, however, most Americans understand little about the functioning of government. Without political leaders to keep them informed and motivated, "few people would be able to overcome the "paradox of participation" (107). So the relationship is a symbiotic one. As much as the public needs a prod and information on when and what to do, the legislators need a show of public support to approve and pass controversial legislative initiatives.

At the risk of oversimplifying a complex dynamic, the mutual give-and-take works as follows. The political leaders inside government inform the advocates outside government of their initiatives, the timing of key votes, and the nature, intensity, and location of the turmoil they anticipate during deliberation. The outsiders, for their part, are particularly well equipped to evaluate what it will take to silence public objections, if not win public support, where it counts most, among reluctant constituents who are pressuring their representatives to resist passage of the initiative.

Now more than ever, partially because of accessible, fast communication via toll-free numbers, fax machines, the Internet, and the like, political leaders and ordinary citizens can work hand in hand. The patronage that occurs goes well beyond the financing of fledgling interest groups. The top-down instigation serves the interests of both officeholders and citizens because it expands the conflict and gets the attention of a greater number of participants. The deliberative phase of lawmaking thus also becomes elongated, often stretching over several Congresses. Although some argue that the institution is dangerously slow and indecisive, the outreach allows for the discovery of new solutions and the formation of new combinations of allies and adversaries.

Among the voices that hold sway on Capitol Hill are spokespersons for the president and his policy agenda. While there are many similarities between these advocates and those from private-sector organizations, there are notable dissimilarities that likely affect motives, strategies, and success when it comes to cultivating relationships in Congress.

Advocacy from the Executive Branch

Because the U.S. Constitution calls for separate branches sharing power, the president is in a position remarkably similar to that of a private lobbyist. While the provision for checks and balances grants him some formal authority to veto legislation and negotiate treaties, he has no legitimacy to oversee members of Congress and determine what initiatives they should write into law. And with separation of powers presidents, senators, and representatives are elected by constituents from geographically distinct jurisdictions (e.g., nation, state, and district), ensuring their independence one from the other. So it is that presidents are forced to bargain and plead their way with members of Congress just like everyone else on Capitol Hill (Neustadt 1980).

Even when the party in the White House holds the majority of seats in Congress, there are no guarantees that presidents will get their way (Pfiffner 1994, Davidson 1988). For many reasons, the most important of which is their accountability to different constituents, presidents can not expect their partisan allies at the other end of Pennsylvania Avenue to do their selling for them. Indeed, even with legions of surrogates working on their behalf, presidents meet with legislative success less than half the time (Pfiffner 1994, LeLoup and Shull 1993, Light 1982). And it is not without a struggle that they accrue the number of wins they do.

What presidents have that advantages them sometimes and hurts them at other times, relative to other players, is an elaborate network of subordinates. Bradley Patterson (1980) depicts the key organizational centers of activity as rings of power emanating out from the president. They include the White House staff, the Executive Office of the President (EOP), and the cabinet. To his breakdown I add one additional ring—the federal bureaucracy.[8] As is true in every other sphere of politics, individuals' goals and the institutional settings in which those individuals operate have consequences for advocacy work in Washington. So it is with two classes of executive staff: presidential appointees and career civil servants.

Those advocates in closest physical and ideological proximity to the chief executive are the president's handpicked advisers, administrators, and spokespersons. Located within the first three rings, these appointees are expected to be loyal to the president and his policy agenda. Many are confidants who have proven their dedication and worth: childhood friends, carryovers from the campaign, professional mentors, and colleagues from prior work experiences. These individuals serve at the behest of the sitting president. Their tenure in the best of times ends with a change in presidential administrations. Because, in a sense, their own accomplishments are measured against what their principal accomplishes, we would expect them to be vigilant about preserving and promoting the president's interests. At least two factors, however, can undermine their loyalty. One is the ambition of the headstrong egotists, who tend to gravitate around successful presidential candidates (Pfiffner 1988). The other, a failing peculiar to some cabinet-level secretariats, occurs when the senior executives find themselves in closer alignment with their subordinates' view of their bureau's mission than the president's view. This phenomenon has been termed "going native" and the "cycle of accommodation" (Pfiffner 1988, Nathan 1983).[9]

In anticipation of this well-known difficulty, most recent presidents select their top officials with two criteria in mind: loyalty and competence (Pfiffner 1988, Nathan 1983). Both attributes are necessary because these individuals play very public roles, often reaching large audiences through television appearances and trips to targeted areas around the country. Appearing on *Meet the Press* or *Face the Nation* on any given Sunday are presidential appointees defending the president's programs and actions.

A decidedly less visible group of players, congressional liaison staff members also hold their jobs at the discretion of the president. They appear in the second and fourth rings around the president, operating out of the EOP and the federal agencies.[10] What distinguishes these individuals from the former ring of players are their career backgrounds, expertise, and foci. These are policy specialists hired to conduct most of the routine coordination and negotiation with members of Congress and their staffs. Their role is not a public one. Unlike the presidential aides, they are not involved in mass marketing executive initiatives. Instead, these people are expected to play an exceptional game of inside politics. To succeed they must know (1) the president's legislative goals, both foreign and domestic, (2) the intricacies of the issues, (3) the sources of congressional support and resistance, and (4) the facts and interpretations of the facts that will alter opinions in line with the president's objectives. Because of the nature of the work, presidents often recruit congressional liaisons from Capitol Hill offices.

Finally, in the outermost ring are career civil servants, around three million people, not including armed services personnel. These people work in any of fourteen cabinet-level federal agencies, in Washington offices, and in state branches across the nation. They assist the president with his constitutional obligation to "take care that the Laws be faithfully executed" (Article 2, Section 3 of the U.S. Constitution). Their willingness to follow the programs and priorities of a Republican one term and a Democrat the next is rooted in their recognition of the legitimacy of the system through which a president gains office (appeal to American voters). They take pride in their work and the mission of the agency they work for. As they see it, no one else has the long view of events they have, and no one knows the intricacies of federal regulations the way they do. Through their professionalism and neutral expertise, they see themselves serving as a much-needed moral balancing wheel for the country.[11] Max Weber (1946, 95), renowned for his work in organization theory, heralded the importance of their role decades ago: "The honor of the civil servant is vested in his ability to execute conscientiously the order of the superior authorities. . . . Without this moral discipline and self-denial, in the highest sense, the whole apparatus would fall to pieces."

The career bureaucrats' disinterest in things political is borne out in a recent National Academy of Public Administration (NAPA) study in which presidential appointees commented on the "helpfulness" of their agencies' professionals.[12] At the top end of the scale, attracting 80 percent or more assents, are tasks the professionals perform such as "mastering substantive details," "day-to-day management," and "technical analysis." At the bottom of the list, attracting 42 and 34 percent of agreement, respectively, are "liaison with Congress" and "anticipating political problems."

These data, together with what is generally reported on the disparity in the working styles of bureaucrats and presidential appointees, suggest that bureaucrats and presidential appointees behave differently toward members of Congress. I expect the latter to behave in a fairly unconstrained manner in locating willing stewards of the president's cause. During the period covered by this study, their openly political connections to Republican President Ronald Reagan, furthermore, may reveal more liaisons with Republicans than with Democrats. In a similar vein, I expect to find that, more than anyone else in the pressure community, Washington-based bureaucrats, the only bureaucrats surveyed, will respond to inquiries from the Hill more than initiate interactions themselves.

Their precise locations in government agencies (e.g., Housing and Urban Development, Education, Agriculture) parallel the committee divisions in Congress (e.g., Housing and Urban Affairs, Education and Labor, Agriculture). If for no other reason than their shared policy mandates, therefore, I expect some executive personnel to favor relationships with some House insiders and not others. Some initial tests of these considerations follow. More elaborate analysis, comparing who works with whom across sectors, is available in the next chapter, on access.

Propositions

Several patterns in organizational involvement are consistent with the individual and institutional incentives and disincentives that are at work in the selective benefits and political patronage theories of political advocacy. First, I expect occupational groups to be the most numerous groups. These are the groups with the resources (e.g., preexisting audiences and infrastructures) to ease their entrée into political advocacy. Next, disassembling the entire sample into six different pressure communities (one for each policy) ought to produce different patterns of group involvement. In keeping with Hansen's observation that interest groups mobilize to protect themselves from harm, I expect the policies that are directed toward regulating an ongoing industry or service (farm credit, trade, and omnibus drug) to awaken larger numbers of occupational than cause-oriented groups. Where I anticipate citizen groups to play a sizable and perhaps dominant role, by comparison, is in the two policy areas that aroused public attention over the proper role of government (e.g., funding the war in Nicaragua and taking the lead in curbing nuclear tests). Welfare reform triggered changes in the established order that threatened government service providers in particular, and it called into question ideological feelings about what to do about the nation's poor. Of all the issues, I expect welfare reform to bring out large numbers of advocates from both occupational and nonoccupational (citizen) organizations.

Profiles in Action: The Evidence on Participation

For two reasons, I adopt an interest-group classification scheme that closely resembles the one used by Jack Walker (1991). First, knowing that the mix of participants in this study ($N = 97$) resembles to a large extent the participants in Walker's survey of the pressure community ($N = 863$)[13] goes far toward affirming that this selection of organizations adequately resembles all organizations that engage in advocacy. (See appendix 1 for a discussion of the sampling procedure.) Second, the breakdown is compatible with my theoretical argument that resources matter a great deal when group organizers compete for political activists. As Walker did, I distinguish between occupational and nonoccupational (cause-oriented) groups. Within the occupational sphere, I distinguish between for-profit and nonprofit organizations.

What is different about the following classification system is the inclusion of administration officials and the initial delineation of public (i.e., governmental) and private-sector organizations. Because some local and state-level governmental associations are indistinguishable from private nonprofit occupational groups (e.g., the Brotherhood of Police Officers and the American Federation of State, County, and Municipal Employees are affiliates of the AFL-CIO), these two categories are subsequently collapsed into one nonprofit category. It serves my interest at the outset, however, to determine the relative level of public and private-sector participation in political advocacy.

Table 3.1 breaks down by organizational classification all the advocacy groups known to have taken a promotional stand on one or more of the six issues under investigation and the subset of sampled organizations that participated in the study. The distributions serve two purposes: (1) They demonstrate the adequacy of the sample to represent the full complement of participating groups, and (2) They depict the relative visibility of different types of organizations.

First, notice that the sample approximates the population in terms of the public-private breakdown, with nongovernmental participants representing 63.5 percent of the pressure community to the government's 36.5 percent in each case.[14] From within the private sector, 83 nonprofit organizations (e.g., professional and trade associations, labor unions, and the like) emerged to press their causes. They comprise 20.7 percent of the 400 groups identified in the entire pressure-group community and 18.6 percent of those interviewed. The for-profit category, which includes multipurpose law firms, corporations, and farmer cooperatives, reaches 15.5 percent representation in the sample compared with 13.0 percent in the population. The citizen component, which includes the cause-oriented groups, has 29.8 percent representation in the population and 28.9 percent in the sample. Within the public-sector category, administration representatives have the most visible presence. And because all promotional organizations that are not citizen-based, cause-oriented assemblies are occupational in nature, by the process of elimination we see that the occupational groups numerically dominate the two distributions, the population (70.2 percent) and the sample (71.1 percent).

What the table does not reveal is the plethora of perspectives, methods, and interests that characteristically reside within so-called homogeneous group types. Federal agencies are renowned for warring over the details of legislative language that threatens to favor one agency at the expense of another in terms of budgets and rule-making authority. In much the same way, governors and state-level associations have vested parochial interests that often spawn competition over federal dollars and regional autonomy.

The multiplicity of interests from within the state and local arenas

TABLE 3.1. Participating Advocacy Group Organizations by Sector and Type

Sector	Population N	Population (%)	Sample N	Sample (%)
Private				
profit	52	13.0	15	15.5
nonprofit	83	20.7	18	18.6
citizen	119	29.8	28	28.9
subtotal	254	63.5	61	63.0
Public				
federal administration	109	27.3	26	26.8
state and local	36	9.0	9	9.3
other (foreign)	1	0.0	1	1.0
subtotal	146	36.5	36	36.1
Total valid cases	400	100.0	97	100.0

toward the war on drugs exemplifies the point. While everyone at this level of government wanted to reduce illegal drug trafficking and the social dysfunctions it creates (e.g., crime, addiction, and family disintegration), solutions for attacking the problem differed with the groups' professional and occupational orientations.[15] In order to catch more drug offenders, police officials lobbied for more money for patrolling the streets.[16] Prison officials argued instead for funds to enlarge rehabilitation programs as a way to halt the rate of recidivism.[17] Budget-conscious lawmakers would have to reconcile the competing interests.

The private-sector occupational groups are also diverse and prone to possess widely divergent attitudes about government initiatives. Among the for-profit organizations, for example, are small and large corporations, ranging from solo consultants in private practice to multimillion-member corporations such as American Express and AT&T. The law firms are domestic and international in scope, including William and Jensen, O'Connor and Hannon, and Deloitte and Touche. There are commercial banks and farmer cooperatives, including the First Boston Corporation, the Farm Credit Services of St. Paul, and the Farm Credit Bank of St. Louis.

The nonprofit segment is also varied, serving the interests of truckers (International Brotherhood of Teamsters), manufacturers (Motor Equipment Manufacturers, National Association of Manufacturers), laborers (International Ladies Garment Workers' Union), movie producers (Motion Picture Association), farmers (American Agriculture Movement), and more. The cause-oriented associations, or citizen-based groups, represent diverse ideologies and interests as well. Numbered among these groups, for example, are Citizens for Reagan, Americas Watch, Greenpeace, Neighbor to Neighbor, Freedom House, Common Cause, and the American Civil Liberties Union.

The evidence on the composition of the pressure-group community presented thus far may be summed up with three points. First, publicly sponsored entities—in particular, those affiliated with the president and the executive branch of government—precipitously swell the pressure community that emerges to battle over national policy. These entities are customarily omitted from investigations of interest-group politics. Second, to no one's surprise, occupational groups dominate nonoccupational groups. And third, even the most narrowly construed organizational classification embodies enormous diversity of purpose, method, and perspective.

That the occupational groups outnumber the nonoccupational groups three-to-one, as they do in this distribution, tells us that the selective-benefits explanation of organized political participation is sound. Had the distribution been lopsided in the opposite way, giving the citizen groups a three-to-one advantage, the data would have seriously challenged the rational perspective and bolstered more resource-neutral constructions of political participation.

In part, the occupational groups have the upper hand because they have the most resources with which to overcome citizen apathy. They have built-in communications systems, ready-made constituencies (e.g., similar educational backgrounds, career interests), and career-appropriate reward structures (e.g., technical information memos, insurance subsidies, high-profile positions, conferences). The cause-oriented groups are disadvantaged in the competition for members because they lack a ready-made constituency, to say nothing of the challenges they face in marketing their causes and the benefits they have to offer responsive citizens.

There is one additional disparity in terms of the challenges that groups face in organizing for political action. Whereas citizen groups cannot function without members (because members legitimate their petitions to government), occupational groups can. Prominent leaders from business and industry speak with authority on what they anticipate will be the costs and benefits to domestic and international markets if policy is changed in a particular way. The individuals for whom they speak may be largely passive on the subject. Or, in the case of corporate moguls, there may be no "members" at all.[18] Thus, the groups that are the most needy in terms of amassing a constituency to legitimate their mission are the citizen-based, cause-oriented groups with the largest hurdles to overcome to convert political spectators into political participants.

Having the numerical advantage in itself is no guarantee of power, however. The diversity of institutional perspectives, if it gives way to conflict, undermines group influence, whether or not the conflict infects different organizational types. So the substantive implication of the preponderance of occupational groups is not yet clear.[19] With the panoply of voices evidenced thus far, it would appear that no one has a clear advantage.

Next, I disaggregate the entire sample into six different pressure communities (one for each policy) to see if the groups' activity levels vary from one policy to another. Given earlier discussions of the incentives that attract members to different organizations and the homogeneity or heterogeneity of the pools from which individuals are drawn, certain patterns are likely. For example, occupational groups, which have comparatively homogeneous memberships (e.g., individuals with similar training and career interests), should mobilize around their spheres of work, taking advantage of opportunities for promoting extended rights and resources at some times and safeguarding against governmental incursions into their turf at other times. Citizen groups, which draw members from all walks of life, are heterogeneous relative to occupational groups. As a consequence, their activity should center on the stated purpose that underlies their members' shared personal convictions (e.g., the organization's mission).

The diversity of jurisdictional perspectives within the public sector suggests one additional pattern. What threatens presidential autonomy is not likely to threaten state and local autonomy and vice versa. Thus, I anticipate discrepancies in the activity levels of administration officials relative to the representatives from other levels of government that are consistent with the participants' occupational self-interests.

Table 3.2 displays the involvement levels of different categories of groups under specified conditions of interest. If there were no rhyme nor reason to the way groups participate in politics, we would predict fairly uniform involvement across the issues on a par with the organizations' share of the entire pressure community. Any variation from those figures (roughly 71 percent for the occupational groups, 16 percent for the for-profits, and 36 percent for the public organizations) suggests that something else is going on. Table 3.2 contains many such variations, all consistent with our theoretical musings.

Taking the occupational connection first, notice that the organizations that draw members from work settings do as well or better than their overall high rate of involvement (71.1 percent) on four of the six issues. In keeping with our expectations, these are the legislative initiatives that most threatened an ongoing industry or service (farm credit, omnibus drug, omnibus trade, and welfare reform). The pattern is partially explained by the activity of the for-profit organizations. While those groups comprise only 15.6 percent of the entire sample, they account for 47.1 percent and 26.7 percent of the activity on farm credit and trade, respectively. In the case of farm credit, the participants included farmer cooperatives, com-

TABLE 3.2.   Issue Involvement by Organization Types (in percentages)

Organization	Total	Contra Aid	Omnibus Drug	Farm Credit	Nuclear Test Ban	Omnibus Trade	Welfare Reform
Occupational	71.1	18.7	85.7	100.0	58.8	93.3	70.6
For-profit	15.6	6.3	0.0	47.1	0.0	26.7	11.8
Citizen	28.1	81.3	14.3	0.0	41.2	6.7	29.4
Public	36.5	6.3	64.3	11.8	52.9	33.3	52.9
Administration	27.1	6.3	42.9	11.8	52.9	33.3	17.6
Valid cases = 96, missing cases = 1							

Note: These figures do not sum to 100 percent because many of the categories overlap. Two categories that are mutually exclusive and therefore sum to 100 percent are the occupational and citizen group types.

mercial banks, and insurance companies, each of which had something to gain from the pending changes. On omnibus trade, the foremost participants from the category include large corporations, such as American Express and AT&T, and law firms representing domestic and foreign companies that were particularly concerned with provisions having to do with expanding their access to foreign markets and limiting the dumping of foreign products in the United States.

On the omnibus drug, test ban, and welfare issues, almost all the observed occupational activity stems from the public sector. Table 3.2 reports two sets of figures. The row labeled *Public* combines the activity of all three levels of government—national, state, and local. The row labeled *Administration* sets the administration officials apart from the rest, reflecting their 27.1 percent share of the pressure community. To see the occupational nature of the involvement of these groups and the extent to which their interests deviate from one another, one need only take account of which jurisdictions dominate which issues and why. I discuss the three issues in which the public-sector groups were most visible—omnibus drug (64.3 percent), test ban (52.9 percent), and welfare reform (52.9).

In the political activity over the Family Support Act of 1988, state and local participants dominated administrative spokespersons two-to-one. For this interpretation compare two figures, the one reflecting overall public-sector involvement (52.9 percent) and the one reflecting exclusive administrative involvement (17.6 percent). As was true of everyone who participated in this debate, the participants sincerely wanted to break the cycle of dependency, which they associated with the dysfunctions of the current program. Governors, human service commissions, and social service providers sought as well to ensure that whatever was done at a national level to modify welfare would neither interfere with their capacity to deliver service nor burden them with new unfunded federal mandates.[20]

When it came to setting out the provisions for the war on drugs, one-third of the groups came from local police departments and correctional facilities, and two-thirds of the public participants represented federal agencies, such as the Justice Department, the U.S. Coast Guard, the National Institute on Drug Abuse, and the U.S. Drug Enforcement Agency.

The policy to restrict nuclear tests to 1 kiloton from the legally permissible level of 10 kilotons aroused no activity from state and local governments. Rather, the participants in this category came wholly from the executive branch of government. They included the Departments of Defense and Energy, their subsidiary scientific laboratories in New Mexico and Arizona, the U.S. Arms Control and Disarmament Agency, and the Joint Chiefs of Staff, to name a few. These were the agencies and indi-

viduals with the technical know-how to both advise the president and promote his interests in Congress.

In all, administration officials overshadow other public-sector politicos on three matters—Contra aid, test ban, and omnibus trade. (Indeed,
here the only governmental players are from the administration: table 3.2.)
In every case the president's power was challenged, but in no case was
executive autonomy more at stake than over omnibus trade. For the first
time in the nation's history we were experiencing a sizable trade deficit,
and legislators were displeased with what they construed to be presidential
mismanagement. To correct the problem, they envisioned devising an
orderly set of procedures that would direct administrative behavior in
dealing with offending countries (Wehr 1988).[21]

Administration officials perceived the legislative initiative as a serious
threat to the president's autonomy, and they dominated the public-sector
scene as a consequence.[22] Defending the president's interests were the U.S.
Trade Representative, officials from the Departments of Treasury, Commerce, and State, and negotiators from the White House.

From the preceding analyses, it is evident that much of the variation
in the political participation of groups pertains to the organizations' occupational orientations and interests. Furthermore, the nonoccupational
groups, which mobilize around shared values toward a cause, are most
numerous on the two issues that turned on matters of moral judgment
about the proper role of government more than on alterations in occupational rights and resources. Only in these campaigns (Contra aid and test
ban) do citizen groups excel, comprising 81.3 percent and 41.2 percent,
respectively, of the mobilized pressure community as compared with their
28.1 percent showing overall.

Next, we examine the proposition that the participation rates of different classifications of groups are sensitive to the subject matter of the
debate, its technical complexity and scope of application, and the extent to
which the issues amass attention in the media (public salience). For two
reasons, the conflict category discussed in chapter 1 is omitted. First, all
the bills arouse a modicum of conflict, making it impossible to observe
behavioral differences when the attribute is missing. Second, on the two
issues in which conflict became public—omnibus trade and Contra aid—
mass interest was aroused. Thus, while we discuss the implications of
salience on political participation, we cannot disentangle the effects of
conflict and salience in each of these situations. The remaining variation is
sufficiently uncorrelated across policies to observe for connections
between the political participation of groups and the issues that embody
these characteristics—complexity, scope, and salience.

Table 3.3 presents the statistical likelihood that the proportionate differences in group activity could have occurred by chance. There are two sets of figures in each cell. The proportion of involvement by the groups possessing the identified classification is compared with the proportion of involved groups not sharing the category label.

The data reveal an important new finding. The involvement of advocacy groups varies with the characteristics of the issues that are under consideration, in particular their scope and public salience. What is more, the direction of these effects is not uniform across the board.

Taking the information on scope first, we see that two types of organizations experience dramatic increases in their rates of participation when issues are broadly construed. Nonprofit occupational groups and those from the public sector eclipse almost two-to-one other promotional groups on the scene at the time. While keeping pace relative to their starting point in the distribution (28.0 percent), citizen groups are vastly outnumbered by their occupational complement (28.6 percent versus 55.9 percent). Only when the issues capture extraordinary media attention

TABLE 3.3. Difference of Proportions: Organization Type by Issue Complexity, Scope, and Public Salience

Organization Type	N	Complexity (%)	Broad Scope (%)	Public Salience (%)[a]
Public				
No	61	37.7	37.7	41.0**
Yes	35	31.4	65.7*	17.1
For-profit				
No	81	32.1	49.4	32.1
Yes	15	53.3	40.0	33.3
Nonprofit				
No	69	37.7	40.6*	36.2
Yes	27	29.6	66.7	22.2
Citizen				
No	68	39.7	55.9*	25.0*
Yes	28	25.0	28.6	50.0
Administration				
No	70	32.9	45.7	35.7
Yes	26	42.3	53.9	23.0

Note on significance: $* p < .05, p \leq .001$.

[a]The proportions reveal activity levels when the condition (complexity, scope, and salience) holds.

Complexity includes farm credit, test ban, and omnibus trade. The texts of these bills and the controversies they engendered include highly technical language.

Broad scope includes welfare reform, omnibus drug, and omnibus trade. The potential that these issues hold for affecting sizable audiences within society is reflected in the above average number of indexing terms they attract in the Library of Congress's on-line system for locating legislative initiatives.

Public salience refers to the action that surrounded the two initiatives—contra aid and omnibus trade—that received above average numbers of articles in the media.

(salience) does the rate of citizen-group participation exceed that of other groups, 50.0 percent and 25.0 percent, respectively. Also when issues are salient public-sector entities appear to suffer the consequences. Their involvement recedes to an all-time low of 17.1 percent.

The connections demonstrated here between organized promotional activity and the nature of the issues makes sense when you reflect on the membership base of various advocacy operations. Take first the correspondence between the policy's breadth and the political involvement of groups. Broad-based national legislation inevitably affects diverse occupational groupings throughout the country. It stands to reason; the broader the reach the more numerous the players. Clinton's plan for healthcare reform triggered myriad reactions from countless sources, in no small measure, I think, because the proposal threatened an industry that comprises one-seventh of the U.S. economy. In the issues under study the two omnibus bills and welfare reform help illustrate the point. Advocates with occupational interests intervened in large numbers because in each case they correctly perceived both opportunities and challenges to the distribution of rights and resources with which they were accustomed.

There is an easy explanation as well for the connection between the record-high turnout of citizen-groups and the saliency of issues. For three reasons citizen groups are particularly susceptible to the interest that policies inspire within the populous. First, when it comes to attracting new members, the group's mission may be decisive in persuading an individual to join one outfit and not another. This scenario is extremely likely when groups have comparable stores of selective benefits to bestow on their prospective members, and the only difference is the policies the groups foster. The groups with the most compelling agenda should have the greatest appeal. Issue saliency comes into play again when group organizers prod their grass roots members to lobby Congress or to write letters to the editors of their local papers. Only when their interest is peaked will group members take the time to respond as directed. Third, lobbyists like to boast of a large citizen base. Whether active or not, it grants them a degree of credibility in the eyes of the officeholders. By contrast, the advocates from occupational groups need none of these emoluments of power that saliency spawns. They need not wait for mass opinion to solidify; it is sufficient that the administrators (and perhaps the members) of the labor union, trade, or professional association are watchful and interested. It is often enough to analyze the economic ramifications of the policy change and produce arguments that resonate with what lawmakers' interpret to be in their own or their constituents' interests, whether or not the issue engenders widespread attention and concern.

The disparities that appear in the column labeled *Complexity* are also enlightening, although their instability warrants caution. It is plausible that citizen-based organizations may be less equipped to intervene over technically complex matters than are their for-profit and executive branch counterparts. Only the cause-oriented groups with specialized knowledge will be equipped to speak with authority on the matter. Other interested citizen groups, because they lack expertise, will be forced to play secondary roles. This is not to imply that the nonoccupational groups cannot educate themselves on the arcana of a complicated issue. They can and do. The Council for a Livable World and Women's Action for Nuclear Disarmament (WAND) are examples of citizen-based groups that have acquired enormous credibility on their subject. The point is that the knowledge they acquired in a dozen years of promotional work is readily available to the scientists who make a living doing research in the area. A mystery that is not so easily explained is the dip in the participation rate of nonprofit groups when issues are complex. Affected occupational groups such as these should have an ample supply of experts on whom to draw in the event that highly technical disputes break out. Definitive statements about this and the more stable associations revealed in table 3.3 necessitate additional analyses of the involvement of organized groups over numerous ventures that vary systematically in terms of their complexity, scope, and salience.

In reviewing all the evidence to this point, in every case save one (Contra aid), there is a noticeable economic motivation to participation. Owing in part to the fact that broad-based national legislation is not market neutral, advocates' professional or occupational interests coincide with the potential for change they see in the legislation. As a consequence occupational and professional interests vastly outnumber nonoccupational interests. Furthermore, public-sector groups emerge to protect their autonomy just as private-sector groups do. What is more, the activity of politicos from within the spheres of government waxes and wanes in line with their professional interests. Because what threatens the autonomy of the executive branch is often different than what threatens the autonomy of state and local officials, these participants trade places dominating public-sector participation. Last, variations in the promotional activities of groups correspond with the scope and salience of issues. The participation rates of public-sector groups and citizen-based organizations fluctuate the most. The administration and for-profit entities participate in modest to high amounts regardless of the characteristics of the policies and the attention to the debate.

Based on the evidence presented here, occupational groups have the upper hand in terms of their visibility on the political playing field. In the next chapter, I analyze the extent to which organizational resources and political access perpetuate or neutralize the disparities discussed thus far.

The Theory and Practice of Political Networking Across Organized Groups

Beyond enlightening us on the array of groups that surface in political clashes over public policy, the selective-benefits theory of group formation has two additional applications. These pertain to group leaders' choices over (1) what issues to champion (e.g., broad or narrow policy involvement) and (2) whether to engage in cooperative ventures with other organizations (e.g., coalition behavior). These decisions affect the pluralism of ideas and the nature of conflict in American democracy.

What follows is an exploration of the conditions that promote and hamper networking among groups. Specifically, I define and explain two phenomena common to the study of interest groups—issue niches and coalitions. Subsequent to each of the theoretical outlooks is a review of the evidence specific to these cases.

Organizational Issue Niching

As a matter of organizational survival, interest groups compete among themselves for legitimacy and recognition. Whether group leaders enlist assistance from political patrons external to their organizations or from their own membership base or both, the result is the same: they need tangible proof of their proximity to power and, even more, evidence of their imprint on policy. As I have said before, corporations, private foundations, local governments, trade unions, federal agencies, religious institutions, legislators, private charities, and wealthy individuals supply an important measure of the financial support and intellectual impetus it takes to spawn and sustain interest groups. The outside patrons are selective with their largesse, however. Knowing this, group organizers are under some pressure to avoid entering battles they cannot win and to boast of their successes when they do take a visible stand.

The competition for recognition encourages groups to specialize in narrow policy areas where it is easier to become a technical specialist and demonstrate the legitimacy to intervene. The patrons (foundations, wealthy individuals, and government agencies) "make investments in groups precisely because they are effective advocates for a cause or because they do a good job of representing the interests of a constituency that the patron wishes to see protected or promoted" (J. Walker 1991, 93).

An organizational reputation as an effective voice for this or that concern gains favor with patrons who want to back a winner. Because few groups have the organizational wherewithal to adopt broadly conceived agendas, more often than not group leaders see the wisdom of taking credit for fewer wins over narrower terrains (Browne 1990, Salisbury 1983). Many of the study participants expressed this sentiment, and one example follows.

> When you decide to support an issue, you have to have some chance of winning. It is damaging to support things that go down in defeat. You have to demonstrate that you can win, even if it means carving up what you want into tiny pieces. You have to demonstrate that you can be successful. That's how you gain credibility with members of Congress and with your grass roots. (Interview, May 1, 1991)

There are pressures within the public sector to curtail involvement in narrow policy areas as well. This time, specialization is a consequence of institutional design and not the strategic behavior of economizing group leaders. The policy foci of the public agencies parallel, in large measure, the jurisdictional division of labor found across congressional committees. Administration officials work most closely with the subset of lawmakers who, due to their committee affiliations, are in the business of funding agency programs and monitoring agency accomplishments. These partnerships are formalized and stable.

A final circumstance argues against the emergence of distinct, nonoverlapping organized interests, and this is the scope and complexity of much of the legislation that Congress writes (Davidson 1992; Salisbury et al. 1992; Wehr 1988, 2215). As evidence of this, notice how the recent debate over containing health-care costs called into question existing laws having to do with pharmaceuticals, hospital management, insurance, welfare, crime, small business, and taxation. Labor policies also encroach into several other domains, including education, the economy, civil rights, and civil liberties. Environmental policy straddles far-flung territories as well including industrial manufacturing, agriculture, and energy. To the extent that modern problems have many sources, legislative solutions have many sides. And as more and more congressional committees and federal agencies team up to scrutinize bills that span formerly discrete and narrow policy domains, the appropriateness of the issue-niche conceptualization of political advocacy breaks down.

With the preceding exception noted, I expect most organizations to conserve their resources and cultivate their reputations by focusing attention within narrowly circumscribed issue niches (agriculture, civil rights, defense, and education, for example). In practice, the groups mirror this degree of specialization. Eighty-nine out of the 97 study participants advocated on only one issue before us; four administrative agencies campaigned on two or three issues; two citizen groups campaigned on two issues each; and one nonprofit occupational group campaigned on two issues. The groups' tendency to concentrate their energies on one domain alone conforms to the issue-niche rendering of the pressure-group community. How, then, do groups adapt to the multidomain phenomenon just discussed? One way a group may maintain its focus and have an impact on broad-based policy is to coordinate its efforts with those of other promotional organizations.

Interorganizational Coalition Building

Subject matter specialization within the advocacy community gives rise to interorganizational networking. There are two explanations of this. First, modern-day problems are complicated. To resolve them legislatively, groups regularly interact with one another, sometimes for a decade or more before the policy is passed.[23] The second reason groups may choose to join forces with one another has to do with the broad focus of so many omnibus measures and the pressure that group organizers are under to use their resources wisely (Hojnacki forthcoming, Hula 1995, Laumann and Knoke 1987). Promotional groups, which specialize in different issue domains, may team up with one another to cover all the congressional bases that need to be covered and work with the individuals with whom they have established trust and rapport (Salisbury et al. 1987).

Using the experiences of the study participants as a guide, we explore the nature and incidence of coalition formation in the pressure-group community. First, in keeping with the scholarship on this subject (Salisbury 1990, Berry 1989, Schlozman and Tierney 1986, King 1978), we see fewer formal coalitions than informal ones. Examples of the formally incorporated groups of groups, having written charters and dues structures, include the U.S. Comprehensive Test Ban Coalition, Countdown 87, the U.S. Chamber of Commerce, and the Business Roundtable. These organizations represent less than 5 percent of coalition activity.

Numerous ad hoc coalitions emerged over the six policies before us. During peak periods in the life cycle of the legislation, many members of these groups report meeting weekly (and sometimes daily) to share information and coordinate their liaison with members of Congress. Examples of these groups include the Central American Working Group (CAWG), the Law Enforcement Steering Committee (LESC), the Center for Defense Information (CDI), the Telecommunications Taskforce (TT), and the Coalition.

While their memberships vary considerably from one coalition to the next (e.g., all citizen-based, cause-oriented groups, such as CAWG; all public nonprofits, such as LESC; a mixture of for-profit and trade associations, such as TT; and a mixture of private nonprofits and citizen groups), these groups of groups universally (1) exchanged information among themselves, (2) kept members of Congress apprised of their research on the issues, as well as their knowledge of the politics—who (officeholder) was leaning this way or that—and (3) received reports from officeholders and staff on the internal political dynamics that could be instrumental in maximizing their lobbying efforts. A spokesperson from the American Friends Service Committee (AFSC) describes the manner in which the coalition members worked with one another and with members and staffers in the House.

> CAWG was indispensable to learn and to share. We met weekly with key officeholders and staff. Normally congressional staff would come and share information on legislative scheduling, the responses they were getting from the executive branch, and what they anticipated was going to happen in the Rules Committee. Also they took reports from us, people off the Hill, to find out what we were discovering on our own. We were a valuable resource to check the swing votes and to get a feel for the direction they might go. Sometimes we would have a speaker from the region come back and give a report on the diplomatic scene. Sometimes we would just share information. (Interview, April 24, 1991)

The beneficiaries of these relationships are the coalition members and the congressional leaders with whom they work. All the advocates who participated in such working groups emphasized the net gains they received from working with other groups. In commenting on the advantages of coalition work, the respondents emphasize their own effectiveness in being able to lobby more members of Congress. In addition, they report that the congressional leaders with whom they work like the technique because it is an efficient use of their champions' time.

Two additional functions were described by a minority of coalition members. On both Contra aid and test ban, citizen groups used their coalitions as headquarters for educating and mobilizing their grass roots members as well as the mass public. A spokesperson from the Council for a Livable World (CFLW) reflected on their role in the test ban coalition.

> CFLW became the clearinghouse [for the coalition]. We [coalition participants] met weekly with several [House] members pertaining to

nuclear test ban. We put together a list of early sponsors and recruited new cosponsors. We developed categories of people—the supporters, the possible supporters [i.e., the undecided], and the definite no's. We played a major role. We even maintained a telephone hot line for people to call in and get information on what was going on pertaining to this issue in Congress. (Interview, June 13, 1991)

In comparison with the pervasive acknowledgment that groups share resources, information, and insights through ad hoc coalitions, relatively few respondents described the coordination extending to the level of centralizing decisions over which advocate works with which member of Congress. According to one spokesperson from the American Public Welfare Association (APWA), which was a member of the Coalition, their leaders capitalized on the preexisting rapport certain coalition partners had with certain House committees.

Rather than having the APWA work directly with members from Education and Labor [not a typical congressional linkage for the group], we targeted liberal-leaning organizations like the Children's Defense Fund and the National Business Association to work there. We had some rapport with members on Ways and Means, so it made sense for us [APWA] to go there. Coalition leaders attempted to match advocates with the House members and staff they had worked with in the past. (Interview, September 13, 1992)

This sort of coordination is feasible only when the coalition embraces groups that represent different political views or focus on different issue domains. Only then can they mastermind targeting (1) liberals to talk with liberals and conservatives to talk with conservatives, or (2) civil liberties groups to talk with members of the Judiciary Committee and tax groups to talk with members of Ways and Means.

Having discussed what coalition leaders value about interorganizational coordination, we can now examine the frequency with which coalitions emerge. The proportion of respondents that places a high premium on the merits of their coalition work varies considerably from issue to issue and from one organization type to the next. For example, a high degree of collaboration occurred over farm credit and aid to the Contras, with 80 percent and 76.5 percent of the respondents, respectively, speaking at great length about their efforts to coordinate with others. Three other policies reveal a middling level of informal group-to-group networking—omnibus trade (53.3 percent), test ban (44.4 percent), and welfare (43.8 percent).

The groups that assembled over omnibus drug reveal the lowest level of collaboration of all (21.4 percent).

In speculating on the factors that could contribute to this variation in organizational behavior, I can think of three possibilities. First, it is plausible that the one-month time period during which the antidrug measure was debated and passed precluded the emergence of interorganizational networks. Second, the Contra and trade bills received the most widespread and sustained media attention, suggesting a positive association between coalition formation and the salience of an issue. Third, trade and welfare reform were referred to numerous congressional committees, perhaps spurring groups to coordinate their efforts with other groups as a way of coping with the vast number of congressional leaders. None of these explanations, however, accounts for the high rate of collaboration on farm credit, a measure that was referred to only three committees and received comparatively little press coverage.

Perhaps the answer to this puzzle resides in the types of organizations that comprise each of the six pressure-group communities more than the nature of the issues themselves. When the participants are grouped by organization type, there is a notable variation in which groups do and do not utilize ad hoc coalitions. The advocates from citizen-based associations report working with other organizations at a significantly (probability ≤ .02 percent) higher rate (73.0 percent) than nonprofit (60.7 percent), for-profit (53.3 percent), or administrative entities (29.2 percent).

Two explanations of the disparity of coalition behavior that goes hand in hand with organizational factors come to mind. The first has to do with the purposes and resources of the occupational groups vis-à-vis cause-oriented groups. The second pertains to the structural features of the federal administration.

I have reasoned that coalitions are born of necessity. Advocacy groups coordinate their efforts with other groups as a way of maintaining their subject-matter specialty and economizing limited resources (e.g., personnel and money for lobbying, research, networking with grass roots members, institution building, and the like). Differences in organizational riches, therefore, may account for the observed variation in coalition formation across groups. The published data on the budgets, membership sizes, and staff sizes of the participating organizations produce mixed results.[24] In keeping with my expectations, the groups that enter into coalitions have budgets that are, on average, less than two-thirds the size of groups that do not use coalitions, and the difference of means is unlikely to occur by chance (probability ≤ .05). Other measures of organizational wealth reveal no strong patterns, however, and thus undermine the logic that coalitions go hand in hand with economic necessity. For example, those with and without large member bases are equally likely to engage in the practice of coalition formation. And while there seems to be a positive association between coalition behavior and organizational staff size (on average, the groups that collaborate have four times as many staff as those that do not), the difference of means does not reach conventional levels of statistical confidence (e.g., probability ≤ .05).

When it comes to explaining collaboration, or the lack thereof, within the executive branch of government, bureaucratic structure, professional roles, and competition for federal dollars may come into play. Many (41 percent) of the respondents from the administration are career civil servants. Their role as neutral experts limits the amount of advocacy in which they engage. As they tell it, they educate legislators who are unfamiliar with the issues, and they provide briefings and analyses to that end. They eschew collaborating with other agencies and organized interests in the private sector because the professional culture to which they subscribe dictates a purely responsive approach to Congress's needs for information. Nothing in the participants' descriptions of their advocacy departs from this picture.

In contrast, political appointees (including White House staff, congressional liaisons, and top executive branch officials) are proactive. Forty-six percent of these individuals, as compared with 25 percent of civil servants, collaborate with their counterparts in other agencies. On the contra issue, presidential lobbyists worked out of the White House, the State Department, and the Central Intelligence Agency (CIA). According to a high-ranking official who operated out of the State Department, there were daily discussions among the president's surrogates (interview, April 2, 1991). On omnibus trade, the job of coordinating all relevant agencies was assigned to one congressional liaison staff member who operated out of the White House (interview, June 24, 1991). Administrative coordination over farm credit was similarly centralized and well orchestrated. According to a principal from the Farm Credit Administration: "We thought it would be a good idea for the folks at Treasury to spearhead the action because they could stand tough against the powerful private interests in agriculture."[25] In other policy areas, executive branch officials do not speak of their collaboration with other agencies. The absence of references to coalition work in other policy areas is either an actual reflection of the paucity of centralized strategies in these cases or an unlucky sampling of administrative officials who were not privy to the coordination that did take place.

Now the variation in coalition formation across issues makes more sense. Citizen groups dominated the Contra fight, and they engage in coalitions at a very high rate. Nonprofits and for-profits use coalitions a middling amount, and the issues in which they dominated (trade and farm credit) reflect a middling level of interorganizational networking. The two policies (drug and test ban) with the highest incidence of administrative participants, the advocates to engage the least in the practice, have the lowest and third-lowest levels of coalition formation. Acknowledging that the paucity of coalition work on welfare reform remains somewhat of a mystery, it looks as if collaboration corresponds more with *who* participates than *what* they rally around (i.e., the scope and complexity of the issue). This interpretation of events challenges much of the assembled wisdom on coalition activity (Browne 1990, Laumann and Knoke 1987, Salisbury et al. 1987, and Schlozman and Tierney 1986), suggesting that more work on the topic is warranted.

In attempting to discern what it is about organizations that predisposes them toward coalition work, norms and resources offer promising lines of inquiry. The depressed levels of coordination among public-sector organizations is no doubt linked in this study to the presence of career civil servants. They leave the task of developing interagency stratagems to deal with Congress to the presidential appointees who hold the "political" jobs. In the private sector, the groups with less-than-average supplies of money are the ones most likely to join forces with other groups. And while these data show no relationship between coalition formation and membership size, and only a weak positive relationship with staff size, I contend that more investigation is warranted before we abandon these explanations of events.[26] If it can be confirmed that an organization's store of staff and active members bears on its decision to join forces with other groups, policy champions in Congress will know where to look for the economies of dealing with a small number of key players who speak for large cross sections of affected communities—citizen-based, cause-oriented groups and nonprofit occupational groups. These, after all, are the only promotional entities with sizable numbers of staff and members.

Summary and Conclusions

The evidence on organizational involvement in promotional politics is overwhelmingly consistent with the rational perspective on political advocacy. For example, the most numerous groups in the pressure-group community have an occupational orientation. This finding gives weight to the argument that individuals join groups for a variety of reasons, only one of which pertains to pursuing a valued cause. Satisfying individuals' needs for additional benefits, whether they are material, solidary, purposive, or some combination of the three, requires institutional resources and administrative skills that preexisting occupational groups have in large supply.

When the participants are broken down into six different pressure-group communities (one for each policy), furthermore, the proportionate changes in organizational involvement vary predictably with what the groups expect to gain or lose. Occupational groups, for example, dominated the scene only when new provisions threatened to alter the status quo of an ongoing industry or service (farm credit, trade, and omnibus drug). The citizen groups, for their part, dominated only one issue, Contra aid, which posed no threat to American business. This and the other instance in which citizen groups represented a substantial share of the pressure-group community (the fight over limiting nuclear tests) turned on philosophical and not economic considerations. In each case, the cause-oriented groups rallied around strong convictions about how they wanted our government to behave. Even the visibility of public-sector groups conforms to the logic that self-interest was at play. Presidential lobbyists outnumber state and local public-sector representatives on the issues that threatened the chief executive's autonomy—omnibus trade, test ban, and Contra aid. The policy that promised to have sweeping ramifications for state and local officials was welfare reform, and this initiative more than any other drew out large numbers of state and local officials and their trade and professional associations.

There are two main findings from this analysis of the correspondence between organizational participation and the characteristics of pending policies. Contrary to conventional wisdom, which holds that occupational groups dominate, these data indicate that promotional organizations jockey for the numerical upperhand. Citizen groups dominate when issues capture extraordinary attention in the media, just as occupational nonprofits do when pending initiatives are broadly construed. The organizations that fluctuate the least in terms of their visibility on the political stage are two types that are not dependent on arousing a member-base for their promotional activity, the for-profit corporations and executive agencies. Second, if the evidence from these six cases is a guide, the scope and saliency of policies affect promotional politics more than does technical complexity. More data are needed to verify the relevance this condition holds for group organizers.

Turning to some interorganizational dynamics of political advocacy, we see, first, that the vast majority of groups limit their promotional work to narrowly circumscribed policy areas. The finding corroborates the issue-niche rendering of policy subsystems. The justification for organizational specialization will be further amplified in the next chapter when respondents discuss how their institution's credibility is affected by success. As expected, informal coalitions are prevalent as well. Typically they emerge on an as-needed basis, with the aim of sharing information and coordinating the groups' efforts more than of masterminding which groups work with which legislators.

Furthermore, the variations that occur in coalition work across the six observed policies correspond more to the type of organizations that dominate any one scene than to the nature of either the issues (complexity and scope) or the debate (saliency and conflict) in question. The advocates from citizen-based associations report working with other organizations at a higher rate (76.5 percent) than either nonprofit (60.7 percent) or for-profit occupational representatives (44.4 percent). Administration officials use the technique least of all (21.4). Whereas disparities in the conditions of their employment and their professional roles satisfactorily explain the disparity in coalition work manifest by career civil servants (25 percent) and presidential appointees (46 percent), we look to disparities in organizational resources to explain the behaviors of assorted private-sector groups. Here the message is mixed. The budget data fit our expectations—on average, financially challenged groups engage in coalitions more than well-financed ones. The staff and membership figures are inconclusive, however. We will return to the matter of resources—who has them and with what consequence—in the next chapter when we take up the matter of access.

CHAPTER 4

The Importance of Access

The most valued tactic of all is not so much a tactic as it is a relationship. Lobbyists would prefer not to be the aggressor, bringing pressure to bear on particular targets. The best of all possible worlds is to be in constant contact with policymakers, continually giving them information about the problems facing the group.

—Jeffrey M. Berry

Jeffrey M. Berry argues that there is a better measure of influence than either organizational resources or numerical advantage, two concepts introduced in the foregoing chapter. In his view, what really matters in the struggle for power is *access*—"who gets to see whom." Holding commitment, expertise, and other factors constant, there is surely a qualitative difference between having substantive, ongoing meetings with a nonranking member of a pertinent congressional committee and having the same access to its chair. And while influence may not increase monotonically with every new contact, advocates who have access to a dozen or more influential leaders must be better off than those who have access to just two or three.

Admittedly, the complexity of congressional power politics and the trusting, personal nature of these policy-oriented relationships caution us against speculating about *one* best combination of leaders (such as the ratio of officeholders to aides or the ratio of party leaders to committee leaders) for advancing the advocates' policy preferences. Although there may be some optimal combinations of leaders that will be most influential in steering legislation through the House, the conditions that bring the champions and the advocates together may spawn some strange combinations of House leaders that are effective and nonetheless appreciated by the advocates who engage them.

Background on the nexus between leadership and followership is critical to our understanding of access; I theorize that besides their mutual concern over the pending policy, what binds the participants is an asymmetry of resources. As the House leaders go about the business of wooing reluctant followers, the leaders need something the advocates have—such as information, well-placed political allies, and credible spokespersons with district connections. The advocates, who want a hand in shaping the legislation, ply their resources in return for access. The explanation of who works with whom therefore begins from the premise that the advocates and the leaders each have something to gain from the relationships they enter. Furthermore, because both partners have limited time and resources, they must be strategic in choosing the best allies to further their respective goals.

To the extent that the organizations with the biggest budgets and the largest staffs also offer the best power resources (e.g., district connections, trust, skill, and politically relevant insights), they have advantages over other groups seeking access. However, if these valuable assets are uncorrelated with the organizations' financial wealth, access may be more evenly distributed than critics would have us believe.

With an eye toward bringing new facts to the debate, this chapter examines access and its origins. In laying out the groundwork for the analysis, the next section begins with a description of the ways House leaders build a voting block of supportive officeholders. From the discussion in chapter 1, I anticipate the piecemeal way in which leaders go about attracting support for legislation. Part of their following comes inadvertently. As John W. Kingdon (1981) and others (Sullivan et al. 1993, Matthews and Stimson 1975, Clausen 1973, Cherryholmes and Shapiro 1969) describe the decision-making process, many legislators who are unfamiliar with the ramifications of the pending issue simply take a voting cue either from their previous positions on the subject or from a trusted colleague who is fully versed on the subject. When colleagues are consulted, quite often the cue giver is a senior member of the sponsoring committee, from the same party as the cue taker, and from a district with similar political divisions and pressures.[1]

Converting additional members to the coalition is not easy. Barbara Sinclair (1983) and other students of House leadership (Rieselbach 1992; Canon 1989; C. Jones 1988, 1968; Peabody 1976) describe diverse influence strategies and the resources they require. While most studies focus on the strategies that are adopted by the formal party leaders—speakers, minority leaders, and such—the lessons are relevant for all those who attempt to wield power in the House.

The section entitled "The Resource Connection" delves into nine types of personal and institutional resources that advocates use in opening doors on Capitol Hill. Following the theoretical presentation on the relationship of advocates and their resources to the leaders' struggle for power within the chamber is the empirical evidence. Here I use the data to answer three basic questions:

1. What does the modal leadership network (e.g., overall size, ratio of officeholders to aides, Republicans to Democrats, and so on) look like, and how much does it vary from one organization seeking access to the next?
2. To the degree that there are discernible patterns in the organizations' leadership networks, to what extent do the differences correspond with the resources, both personal and institutional, that the advocates bring to bear in gaining access and the types of groups they represent?
3. How do the advocates assess the "fit" between the realized outcomes and the idealized outcomes they sought to achieve?

Influence: An Elusive Target

The Influence Connection: The House and Its Members

An assumption that runs through this book is that legislators are rational. The perspective is not very demanding.[2] It simply means that officeholders, rather than behaving randomly, have a canny ability to assess reality in terms of their own interests. All it takes is awareness of one's likes and dislikes and common sense.

In almost every case, political scientists do not actually ask lawmakers what they are trying to accomplish. Instead, they observe the way officeholders behave and make inferences about what must have motivated them. Three goals, in particular, have held up well in predicting all sorts of behaviors. In order of their prominence in the literature, they include (1) gaining reelection, (2) making good public policy, and (3) obtaining influence in the chamber.[3] Representatives choose committee assignments (Fenno 1973), shepherd policies (Hall 1992), delegate tasks to staff (DeGregorio 1993), and defer to trusted colleagues for voting cues (Kingdon 1981) in keeping with these goals.

In Congress more than other institutions, leaders lead *only* because followers let them. This is so because there are no authority figures here in the sense of administrators who are hired to render into one harmonious working whole the disparate energies of its 435 component parts. Rather, everyone from the most senior to the most junior member gains admittance to the organization through the same costly and harrowing experience—winning more votes than anyone else in an electoral constituency of about 570,000 citizens. And the incumbents' preoccupation with this rite of passage, which they undergo at two-year intervals, is probably the single biggest threat to building consensus around contentious issues.

Because success at the polls is a necessary precondition for achieving either of the other two goals, making good public policy and gaining influence, incumbents invest a good deal of time and resources in communicating with their constituents. The number and placement of staff in district offices, members' dual residences and weekly trips home, surveys of constituent opinion, periodic newsletters, and solicitations to "help cut the red tape of bureaucracy" are just a few of the practices that officeholders engage in to learn what constituents want and, whenever possible, to take credit for delivering it (Fiorina 1977, Fenno 1978, Mayhew 1974). From the incumbent's point of view, there is no substitute for being held in high regard by their voters. Unfortunately for House leaders who are trying to bring warring factions together around one mutually acceptable set of provisions, a vote for the leadership may be a vote against one's district. With a campaign never more than two years away, House members are prone to side with their constituents, often leaving the leaders short of the majority of votes they need to pass their bills.

Besides the reelection jitters that undermine the leadership's attempts to build winning coalitions within the chamber, a feature of the campaign process itself also thwarts coordinated, centralized actions. For the past thirty years, individuals win their seats with minimal help from either political party. The parties typically contribute about 5 percent of the total campaign dollar in House races, offer in-kind services such as access to television studios, mailing lists for fund-raising, and polling data, and assist with get-out-the-vote drives. While these aids are helpful, they are rarely decisive. Instead, the real engine in the race is the candidate and his or her assembled consultants, confidants, staff, and volunteers. These individuals, not the party operatives, help ambitious politicians sound out their chances of winning (Herrnson 1990, Fowler and McClure 1989). Even when the campaign is under way, these people, working directly for the member, conduct polls, develop campaign strategies, and get the message out to district audiences. Gary C. Jacobson (1992) calls this peculiarly American phenomenon "candidate centered" campaign politics.

The implication for leadership inside Congress is clear. Formal party officials, having little institutional credit to claim for the victories of their rank-and-file members, must cajole rather then command their way to a following (Little and Patterson 1993; Rohde 1991; B. Sinclair 1995, 1992a, 1983; and C. Jones 1988).[4] Thus, leaders gain votes for or against a legislative initiative in a way remarkably similar to the ways interest-group organizers boost membership in their organizations: They seek to anticipate and then satisfy the interests of their targeted audience of followers. In Congress, leaders' strategies are tailored to appeal to legislators' goals to be reelected, to develop good public policy, and to cultivate influence.

Barbara Sinclair (1983) provides a classification system for describing the approaches that the majority-party leadership employs to build coalitions in the House. These approaches include (1) providing services to individuals, (2) manipulating voting outcomes by structuring the rules of procedure, and (3) extending opportunities to participate in decision making. The first and last of these are utilitarian in nature. The leadership parlays favors with the expectation that indebtedness lays the groundwork for compliance. Structuring choice is decidedly coercive. In the elaboration that follows, notice that with few exceptions, majority-party leaders of congressional committees, who are not included in Sinclair's scenario, have rights and resources similar to those used by the Speaker and the majority leader.

Representatives in the U.S. House have a uniquely demanding job. With biennial elections always on their minds, they must take care to succeed at home in their districts as well as in Washington with their colleagues. Those who aspire to leave a personal imprint on national policy or carve out domains of influence over others need room to maneuver away from the critical eye of constituents. They do so, first, by staying out of trouble and voting right on the bills that matter to their constituents. Second, they cultivate trusting, positive relationships with their voters so they are not questioned about every speech, vote, and trip they make when they are out of view of the district (Bianco 1994). Reelection concerns are so predictable and so paramount that they offer opportunities for leaders to ingratiate themselves with potential followers by providing services. When Sinclair (1983) describes *service,* she is speaking about information, positions, campaign support, office space, and staff—tangible resources that help would-be followers succeed in their careers.[5]

Additionally, leaders can schedule votes (majority leader), refer bills (Speaker), schedule hearings (committee chairs), and invite witnesses (committee chairs) to accommodate members' interests and in so doing build indebtedness. What successful coalition leaders really need, then, are (1) resources that can be conferred upon others as benefits, and (2) awareness of the tastes and preferences of the members who are targeted for influence.

The *strategy of inclusion* gives junior (often freshmen) and formally excluded members (those not on a committee of referral) the opportunity to work on an issue through a task force. Speaker Thomas "Tip" P. O'Neill (D-Massachusetts) used this approach to his advantage in the last several years of his rule. By involving more people early on in the legislative cycle and giving them a tangible position from which to take some credit (e.g., member of a task force), he would not only win the votes of his recruits but also gain the benefits of their sales pitches directed at other colleagues.

In 1987 Speaker Jim Wright's Task Force on Central America, chaired by David Bonior, conferred power on many relative newcomers to the institution, who became avid champions of the party's effort to curtail funding the Contras in Nicaragua. This strategy of inclusion, more than the others (service and structure), relies on a blend of utilitarian and normative (educational) mechanisms of control.[6] The more involved a person is in firsthand deliberation and negotiation, the more the participant will understand the complexity of the arguments and feel a sense of ownership with the result. In all likelihood, as well, what Albert O. Hirschman (1970) observed in organizational affiliations generally holds true in Congress. Loyalty to an organized effort increases with the amount of time one devotes to it.

Last, power wielders can force particular outcomes by *structuring choice*. The Speaker, with the assistance of the Rules Committee, provides the most vivid example of this strategy, but any individuals in positions to set agendas have the same kind of power (Krehbiel 1991, Bach and Smith 1988, Riker 1982). One of the most publicly visible accounts of the strategy occurred in the spring of 1993 when House Democrats foiled House Republicans' efforts to modify a budget resolution that had the official backing of the president. "The Republicans were outvoted and outmuscled by the House's overwhelming Democratic majority, limited to just two amendments that they had no chance of passing" (Hager 1993b, 653). Restrictive rules like the one discussed here usually pass in straight party-line votes, and they silence all debate on any options other than the one preferred by the majority-party leadership. A consequence of such coercive tactics rules is they exacerbate cleavages between the parties and threaten the chances for future cooperation between the parties.[7]

In committee, chairs can bury initiatives at several junctures prior to a floor vote, just in the way they structure the decisions of their panels' business. They select from a host of topics the issues that will receive the scrutiny of a public hearing. They choose the witnesses who will testify and in so doing develop the public record on the scope and intensity of the problem as well as its amenability to government intervention. In preparation for bill markup, it is the chair who assembles a working document for all to debate.[8] At every step of the way, committee leaders have the power to advance their own interests and foil those of their adversaries. Instead, they tend to accommodate their colleagues at every turn in the hope that their power will be reinforced and strengthened in the long run through day-to-day demonstrations of their own tolerance and service to others (DeGregorio 1993, Loomis 1988).

In this way, *not* structuring choice becomes a service to colleagues that endears the leadership to them. A wise leader knows when and when not to press reluctant followers. Indeed, veteran lobbyist Charls E. Walker refers to just this skill, when he draws on the Texas gambling song to elaborate his point on the qualities of a good horse: "He needs to know when to hold them, know when to fold them, know when to walk away, and know when to run" (C. Walker 1989).

Advocates and their sponsoring organizations have resources—information, money, contacts—that can help House leaders build supportive coalitions around policies of mutual interest. By investing their time, energy, staff, members, and money in influential leaders, the advocates accomplish two aims: (1) They bolster the influence of the principals who they have estimated to be the most qualified individuals to spearhead their causes, and (2) They insinuate themselves informally in the decision-making process.

The Resource Connection: Organizations and Their Advocates

In keeping with the foregoing discussion of what it takes to build a following inside the House, I expect several organizational attributes to be instrumental in opening doors on Capitol Hill. They include the organization's (1) legal status, (2) campaign involvement, (3) number and location of offices, (4) membership size, diffusion, and ideology, (5) budget and staff, and (6) institutional credibility. The advocates also possess skills and talents that may gain them access apart from what their institutional affiliations afford. Here I am thinking of (1) professional service, (2) personal credibility, and (3) prior experience. I will discuss each of these items in turn.

Legal Status
As we have seen, private, nongovernmental organizations that engage in promotional politics do so as either for-profit or nonprofit entities. For-profit organizations are nearly unconstrained in the strategies they employ to cultivate access with politicians. For-profits may offer campaign contributions (discussed in more detail subsequently) and, budget permitting, maintain an around-the-clock vigil of the political elites who have jurisdiction over their vital interests.

The nonprofit associations, by contrast, have to decide how close they want to get to the political process. Tax-exempt organizations place considerable distance between themselves and the politicians. One type, the 501(c)(3)s, specialize in education and research, keep professional lobbying to a minimum (approximately 15 percent of the organization's overall staff effort), and refrain from campaign work. In exchange for these restraints on their activities, the organizations are free to solicit money from citizen members and organizational patrons who support the group's cause *and* seek a tax shelter in the process. Interest groups with 501(c)(3) status may also receive bequests, which are deductible for estate and gift taxes. And they are eligible for public and private grants that help subsidize the costs of research and administration. Furthermore, large organizations that rely on frequent mass mailings for both institutional maintenance as well as political mobilization save millions of dollars through subsidized postal rates (Shaiko 1992, J. Walker 1991). These are the most prevalent organizations in the interest-group community. Examples include the Food Research and Action Center, Greenpeace USA, and Mothers Against Drunk Driving (MADD).

The nonprofit organizations that are committed to influencing political elites through a sizable lobbying presence and campaign money incorporate as 501(c)(4)s. For the privilege of engaging in these power tactics, the organizations give up all the government subsidies that the tax-exempt groups receive. Examples of these groups include the American Civil Liberties Union (ACLU), Common Cause, and the Center for International Policy. Because there are no legal restrictions to bar a well-endowed organization from piggybacking the two structures together, we see hybrid associations that have a 501(c)(3) research and education arm and a 501(c)(4) lobbying arm. Examples include the National Association for the Advancement of Colored People (NAACP), the National Abortion and Reproductive Rights Action League (NARAL), and the Sierra Club.[9]

The connection between a group's access and its legal status has to do with the extent to which advocates gain exposure to the leaders and the quality and timeliness of their information. I speculate that House leaders will lean heavily on the advocates from for-profit corporations and the non-profit 501(c)(4)s, if for no other reason than these are the people they encounter with the greatest regularity. In comparison, the 501(c)(3) organizations downplay their lobbying efforts and specialize in research and education. Their access, as a consequence of their legal structure and accompanying specialization, is likely to rest primarily on the quality and timeliness of their information. The hybrid associations are in the most enviable positions of all because they have the legal flexibility to offer a full menu of resources to their allies on the Hill.

Campaign Involvement

Most private organizations assiduously avoid involvement in political campaigns on grounds having little to do with their legal status.[10] Group leaders may want to protect their members from the potentially divisive process of choosing to back some candidates and not others. As for those organizations that do provide support, it is immaterial whether the support is an official organizational endorsement, a financial contribution, or the labor of energetic volunteers. Public-sector organizations, however, have little choice in the matter. The Hatch Act bars federal employees from participating in political campaigns.

Two types of advocacy groups become involved in the financial support of political campaigns. The first type are free-standing political action committees (PACs) that do nothing to influence policy outcomes other than to influence the complement of elected officials who make the laws. The National Conservative Political Action Committee (NCPAC), the National Committee to Preserve Social Security PAC, and the Realtors PAC are examples of organizations that have amassed large amounts of money and have successfully targeted their contributions to heighten the proportion of decision makers who show an affinity for the groups' tastes toward public policy (R. Smith 1988). Because these groups do not lobby, they are not represented among the study participants. The second type of PAC is part of a larger operation. While they raise and spend campaign dollars in the hope of constructing a kinder, gentler Congress, their 501(c)(4) affiliates do what they can to create supportive conditions outside the institution (by building an attentive, politically active membership: promoting, for example, a positive presence in the media or in the public at large). Some examples of these partnerships include the Council for a Livable World and Peace PAC, the U.S. Chamber of Commerce and the National Chamber Alliance for Politics, and SANE/FREEZE and SANE/FREEZE PAC.

Political action committees can contribute money to other PACs as well as to individuals.[11] And because House leaders sometimes set up their own campaign fund-raising organizations to serve their colleagues, private PACs play into the leaders' hands by contributing funds to the "leadership PACs."[12] Such a strategy is sure to be remembered favorably by the leaders, who now have more money under their own control with which to build a following. The more funds they receive, the better equipped they are to reward their past political allies and to create indebtedness with would-be supporters (Wilcox 1990, 1989).

While informed observers, scholars, and practitioners disagree over the power of campaign money to buy legislators' votes, there is little disagreement that contributions do buy legislators' time.[13] Campaign contributors, and their affiliates who engage in promotional work, are sure to be granted an initial audience with their now-elected beneficiaries. However, the extent to which this preliminary contact translates into long-term access or supportive votes, I speculate, has more to do with such factors as the quality of the consultation and the persuasiveness of the presentation than it has to do with the size of the donation. That is why it is important to consider nonmonetary resources along with the monetary ones.

Number and Location of Offices

Having a physical presence on Capitol Hill is a valuable asset. The fact that tens of thousands of interest groups have offices in and around Washington speaks for itself. Over and over again, advocates evaluate their access, at least in part, on the basis of their persistence: "You just wait them out." "If you are persistent you can pretty much get in the door with anyone." "I just sat down in the outside lobby and told the receptionist I had five hours to wait. Within a few minutes the chief council (the target of the sit-in) came out laughing, and he met with me."[14] These and comments like them speak to the importance of proximity.

Having a Washington office makes it easier for advocates to survey what is going on from one day to the next within the institution and among the principals. It also greatly facilitates the advocates' capacity to respond quickly to the leaders' often precipitous calls for briefings, documents, strategy sessions, and the like.

Large membership groups often organize as federations with offices in several regions of the country, if not in all fifty states, in addition to their national headquarters in the capital area. The structure benefits the interest group in two ways. First, a federated organization allows its subsidiary groups some freedom to tailor their policy foci and methods of influence to the specific preferences of local members. With regional tastes being as diverse as they sometimes are, this flexibility is necessary for institutional maintenance (Rothenberg 1992, Schlozman and Tierney 1986, J. Wilson 1973). The organizational tolerance that is part and parcel of federal structures keeps members happy and productive. Second, and more to the point of the discussion on access, when professional staff members are located in several locations across the country, the organization is equipped to size up the political situations that the legislators face in these localities and to offer valuable information on alternative ways of bringing ambivalent officeholders on board. Such politically relevant interpretations are valuable to the coalition builders in the House, and some groups are better suited than others to supply these analyses if for no other reason than their geographic locations.

Having even one office in a strategic location can be of immeasurable value in one's quest for access as well. One participant in the debate over the farm credit bill describes the boost in appeal that his link to rural America, the location where so many farm families were at risk of losing their livelihoods, provides him. In his words, "I am a recognized expert in the area, and I am not a Washington 'insider.' In fact, I am from a town of 850 people, and I think it raises my credibility with the members of Congress" (interview, June 23, 1992).

Large corporations, occupational nonprofit groups, and large citizen-based groups may be equally well positioned geographically. So on this dimension we use the data in an exploratory manner, reserving judgment for the time being as to what types of groups are favored.

Membership Size, Diffusion, and Ideology
Groups with large memberships often have several offices, so this and the number and location of offices are linked to some extent. The two assets also offer quite different mechanisms for gaining access. When interest groups publicly endorse a bill, legislators take notice. Size alone matters because it offers a degree of institutional legitimacy. If millions of organized Americans say it is in their interest to pass the omnibus drug bill, for example, undecided officeholders must at least hear out the arguments.

Legislators' appeals for an end to our government's financial support of the Contras fighting in Nicaragua received notice when several large church groups organized with the same goal in mind. All told, the advocates for the United Church of Christ, the American Baptist Church, and the National Council of the Churches of Christ could boast of several million members.

Two other qualities about an interest group's member base give pause to decision makers: one is the group's geographic dispersion, and the other is its political ideology. Organizations that have geographically dispersed members have a tremendous capacity for access. They merely capitalize on the group's district connections. A surefire way to gain access to busy officeholders is to line up a meeting between the targeted lawmaker and one of his or her own constituents, someone who both is engaged in the affairs of the district and is a prominent member of the advocacy group.

Furthermore, when an organizational staff member accompanies the constituent group member, the advocate has an opportunity to demonstrate his or her own talents for analysis and persuasion. Many long and mutually beneficial partnerships between officeholders and professional advocates get their start in this way. What is important is the geographic placement of the group's membership. The more dispersed one's members are, the greater the likelihood that there will be a constituent-legislator match. Moreover, a group's capacity for high-volume, constituent-oriented networking is an asset that can be parlayed into access with the House leaders, who are themselves on the lookout for well-placed political allies.

In selling aspects of the welfare reform bill to rank-and-file members of the House, the leadership was assuredly pleased to be able to invoke the names of several prominent, strategically placed organizations. Consider the political and geographic benefits afforded in the following array of groups as an example: the National Governors Association, the American Public Welfare Association (a group of state welfare commissioners), and the American Federation of State, County, and Municipal Employees (AFSME). For their part, the coalition of organizations could boast of supporters up and down the service line (politicians, top administrators, and direct service providers) from one coast to the other.

Last is the matter of the groups' political ideology. Most promotional organizations avoid siding with one party or the other because doing so limits their maneuverability. However, even so-called nonpartisan organizations develop track records for taking conservative or liberal stances toward the issues they track. For example, the National Tax Payers Union, the Heritage Foundation, and the Hoover Institute have long argued for cuts in taxes and the social programs they support. Other groups such as the Children's Defense Fund, the American Association of Retired Persons (AARP), and the American Council of Education consistently endorse expanding government's service to children and support for education and the elderly (*Public Interest Profiles* 1988).

When congressional leaders attempt to get a long-standing adversary to cooperate with them in passing a bill, what better envoy to make the promotional pitch for them than a kindred spirit and former ally of the targeted legislator who has seen the light and now supports the leadership? Coalition building is greatly facilitated inside the chamber when an outside group that is typically hostile to a particular type of policy turns around and favors it. Such a situation happened in 1990 when business groups began to support clean air policy. Resistant legislators had to reexamine their positions: "If business is for this, and I support business, then I should support this." The same sort of unexpected positioning took place in passing some of the conservative provisions of welfare reform. Heretofore, liberals inside and outside of Congress would abhor work requirements as demeaning for the deserving poor. Yet in 1988 liberal groups such as the Children's Defense Fund supported even conservative aspects of the bill. Their support, according to a spokesperson for the American Public Welfare Association, made it easier for reluctant Democrats to go along with the leadership.[15]

There is much truth to the old adage that "politics makes strange bedfellows." Advocates eager to gain access to leading coalition builders with whom they typically disagree may find that their "different" ideology actually facilitates gaining access.

With time in short supply, as it often is for policy champions both inside and outside the institution, the leaders and advocates can team up and coordinate their efforts. Advocates know the value of their organizations' endorsements and contacts. The most advantaged groups in terms of securing access through these means are nonprofit occupational groups and large, geographically dispersed citizen-based organizations. Groups without large complements of civic-minded volunteers (for-profit organizations and some research institutions) will likely build access on different grounds (e.g., sound and timely analysis and a persistent presence).

Budget and Staff
Of all the resources that an organization can muster to win access, money and staff are surely the most versatile. Staff may be deployed on myriad projects. If available, money and time can be used to (1) conduct targeted public opinion polls, (2) acquire and analyze economic data pertinent to affected districts, and (3) sponsor retreats in which officeholders and community leaders consult with one another in a relaxed setting. When an organization has money and a talented staff, it has enormous potential for access and influence.

Furthermore, if the organization's own staff is incapable of supplying a particular service, special consultants may be paid to do the job. Money and staff can provide nearly everything a political leader needs, except perhaps the added legitimacy that comes with a mass volunteer, citizen-based effort.

For-profit organizations and well-endowed nonprofits, citizen or otherwise, are certainly advantaged when it comes to providing legislators with adjunct staff. We will return to the subject of "professional service" subsequently when we consider the personal assets that advocates use to win access.

Institutional Credibility
Like money, institutional credibility is crucial on Capitol Hill. Legislative leaders may win the support of their colleagues by demonstrating that their bill is backed by organizations that have a reputation for sound judgment and independent thinking. While institutional credibility is unarguably a desirable trait, it is an illusive concept. In part, an organization's credibility is associated with the commitment and talent of its members, administrators, and staff.

With this in mind, we now turn to attributes that are associated with the advocates themselves, their service to members of Congress and their staffs, their prior experience with the issues and the players, and their reputations as clever, credible policy promoters.

Professional Service

Sometimes advocates offer professional services—speeches, issue briefs, policy analyses—to congressional insiders in the hope that they will be remembered favorably and be granted the access they desire with influential legislators and aides. They do this even on matters unrelated to their lobbying efforts. Their sole aim is access. By demonstrating their talents for clear thinking, sound judgment, and hard work, they count on being remembered and called in on issues when their organization's interests are at stake. Over time this strategy could result in a healthy ongoing relationship in which the advocates and the House leaders continually rely on each other for valuable assistance, in part alleviating the advocates' worries about gaining access.

The leaders benefit as well, because when they have known, reliable adjunct staff ready to assist them in their quest for influence, they waste little time in the start-up costs of launching a new leadership endeavor.

Because there are no legal restrictions on advocates assisting their policy champions in this way, all groups can engage in the practice with equal fervor. However, organizations with few professional staff members may not have sufficient resources to detail vital personnel to serve congressional insiders on matters unrelated to the organization's mission. Yet these are the best opportunities for earning future access because there are no institutional conflicts of interest to constrain the advocate's contribution (e.g., analysis and outreach). Staff numbers permitting, 501(c)(3) organizations may be predisposed to use this approach. Advocates from these settings may not benefit from their sponsors' involvement in financing political campaigns, so they may see service as a good substitute for gaining access.[16] The service strategy also makes sense for relative newcomers, regardless of sponsorship, who are trying to establish credibility as valuable players.

Personal Credibility

Although it is difficult to measure the impact of advocates' contributions in terms of policy successes, it is reasonable to think that their congressional partners formulate impressions of the advocates' value to their leadership enterprise. In study after study, advocates speak of the importance of their own credibility (J. Walker 1991, Berry 1989, Schlozman and Tierney 1986). So we can expect that credibility figures prominently in the advocates' explanations of their Hill access.

Another feature that undoubtedly fosters credibility is being correct. Conducting head counts of who will and will not support the leadership's position on an upcoming vote is an activity in which advocates engage that is easily assessed for its accuracy. Several respondents linked their access to Hill leaders to their capacity to arrive at better head counts than the House's own whip system, which is formally charged with the responsibility.[17]

This is another attribute that probably has no particular correspondence with organization type. Perhaps the best people will be attracted to the highest-paying jobs and therefore concentrated in well-endowed organizations (sector notwithstanding), but personal observation suggests otherwise. There are countless examples of extremely creative individuals working for low wages in relatively obscure organizations. Thus I refrain from any prediction and let the data be the guide.

Prior Experience
One final personal asset certainly affects gaining an entrée on Capitol Hill. Call it experience, the old boys' network, or the revolving door, it adds up to the same thing: Leaders work with people they trust. Where the trust is initially established may be immaterial, but we can consider a few options besides the service provision discussed earlier. Many leader-advocate relationships start on Capitol Hill, with the future advocate serving as officeholder or aide. In other instances, leaders learn to trust an advocate after a series of successful ventures with that advocate. Lastly, although this circumstance may be more rare, some advocates become officeholders. When this happens, the officeholder has many positive relations to draw on from past lobbying days. Rosa DeLauro (D-Connecticut) comes to mind as an example—a legislator, elected in 1990, who previously directed Countdown 87, a coalition of organizations that opposed aid to the Contras.

The bottom line is that leaders and advocates need partners they can trust to get the job done, and it would be imprudent to dismiss the role that personal loyalties play in gaining Hill access. Not knowing how these attachments break down by organizational type, however, I use the data in an exploratory fashion to provide some answers.

The organizations and advocates most at odds with the foregoing argument (save the discussion about personal credibility and past experience) are those from the administration. Federal bureaus do not have members or district-level offices in the same way citizen and occupational groups do, and, as we have noted before, the Hatch Act prohibits presidential aides from participating in congressional campaign activity.

An important determinant of executive-legislative liaisons not present anywhere else is the structural link that derives from Congress's formal budgetary and oversight roles vis-à-vis the executive branch of government. The link should be particularly strong for civil servants who develop long-term relationships with the officeholders and staff of the congressional committees that have jurisdictions over their policy domains.

Other predictions are strictly speculative, given the paucity of the information on interbranch politics between members of Congress and advocates from the executive branch. Perhaps presidential appointees will work with a greater number of officeholders than aides, delegating to their subordinates the staff-level outreach. That career civil servants develop long-standing relationships with veteran incumbents suggests a compelling counterargument, however. Their expertise on the issues and their memories of past battles won and lost may make them better allies and confidants than the more transitory, although allegedly powerful, presidential appointees. If this is so, the career civil servants will work with as many officeholders as do the political appointees.

Propositions

In comparing the officeholder-to-staff ratio and overall size of the networks that advocates assemble to promote their policy aims in the U.S. House, I expect that personal attributes of the advocates and organizational characteristics of their institutional sponsors make some groups more appealing than others as they attempt to gain access to leaders on the Hill. My predictions assume that congressional leaders and advocates are purposive in their behavior. The leaders want to influence the officeholders who vote in the House, and they need a variety of resources to bolster their influence. The advocates want to see certain leaders succeed, and they have resources that will help them do so.

Moreover, the institutional settings within which these individuals pursue their interests offer opportunities and constraints that moderate behavior. House leaders must build coalitions through personal and often utilitarian means. Because their targets of influence, the rank-and-file members, are often concerned with reelection, the leaders must get inside the psyches of their would-be followers and figure out interpretations and explanations of policies that will wash with those would-be followers' constituents. The process calls for sophisticated analyses of innumerable disparate situations in areas that are usually geographically remote from Washington.

Advocacy groups that have strategically convenient offices, dispersed members, and well-placed political allies make exceptionally attractive promotional partners for needy congressional coalition builders. In contrast, the advocates who represent comparatively impoverished organizations with limited staff, budgets, and members offer much less to congressional leaders.

This intellectual reasoning yields some propositions about the correspondence between *access* (e.g., who an advocate works with) and *assets* (e.g., the personal and organizational resources an advocate can apply to the policy debate). As assets increase, I expect a corresponding improvement in the nature of the leadership networks—such as larger overall networks, higher proportions of officeholders, and higher proportions of high-profile leaders. To settle, or perhaps reawaken, some concerns over the "upper-class accent" in the interest-group chorus (Schattschneider [1960] 1975, 35), I test the extent to which the access of groups from different organizational sectors can be attributed to differences in their endowment of assets. Last, I explore the data for answers to more speculative questions on which there is little prior research. For example, do private-sector groups construct different leadership networks than public-sector groups, specifically those working for the administration? Are some personal (e.g., valuable prior experience) and organizational (dispersion of offices) assets distributed within the pressure community in such a way that the assets may account for observed differences in access?

The Evidence on Who Works With Whom

The discussion of the findings is in four parts. First, I examine the descriptive evidence on the two components of interest: (1) access, as manifest in the number and type of individuals that advocates include in their leadership networks, and (2) assets, as manifest in the resources that advocates and their organizations bring to bear on the policy process. Second, I test theoretical propositions and answer exploratory questions pertaining to the correspondence between access and assets. Third, I examine the assembled leaders by organization type, seeking insights into the groups' strategies for influencing political outcomes. Last, I compare the advocates' assessments of how well they did in their attempts to bring policy outcomes in line with their own views. In doing so, we learn the relative levels of satisfaction across group types and subsequently discern other ingredients to success.

What Does the Modal Leadership Network Look Like, and
How Much Does it Vary from One Organization Seeking
Access to the Next?

The different dimensions on which to judge the networks are their relative size and composition. At one end of the continuum is a network made up of two congressional staff members and no officeholders. Twelve leaders comprise an average network. Seventy-five percent of these individuals are officeholders, 75 percent have majority-party status (Democrats), and 23 percent hold ranking positions in either the formal party structures or the committees of referral. The most resplendent network is comprised of 44 officeholders and no aides, an average balance of partisans, and uncommonly large shares of committee leaders (45 percent) and representatives from two powerhouse committees—Ways and Means (29 percent) and Rules (18 percent).

The organizational resources that the participants bring to the process are varied as well. Using information on the organizations' staff size, budget, and membership as a guide, two participants in the study are clearly the least well endowed. One is a for-profit consulting firm that is operated by a single agent out of his Washington apartment. The other is a citizen-based group with an undisclosed number of members. The citizen-based group is staffed on a volunteer basis by an individual who also works out of his home. The organization is located on the West Coast and is without an operating budget. The organizational setup that represents the middle of the distribution has an operating budget of $2 million dollars, a staff of 35, and a membership of 7,000. The most financially well-endowed group is an occupational entity with a $65 million budget. The organization with the largest recorded staff (313,000) is a for-profit corporation. And a church-based association has the most members (43 million). That each of the organization types excels in a different measure of institutional wealth reveals a level of diversity that recurs later when we analyze the lobbyists' interpretations of what brings about access.

Are There Patterns Between the Classifications of Advocacy Groups and the Types of Resources They Have to Apply in Gaining Access?

Table 4.1 breaks down the data on the personal and organizational assets discussed in the previous section by group type. The first part of the table includes data taken from published sources on budget, staff, and membership. Because federal employees in the executive branch have access to members of Congress by virtue of their positions in the administration, attributes having to do with the agencies' budgets and staff have limited value for our purposes and are not presented. Four additional organizations withheld information on these dimensions, reducing the total number of groups in this display to 65. Only the percentages for the resource-rich (median and above) strata of groups are included. The groups with below average shares of each resource make up the balance in each cell. The participants' assessments of the value these and other attributes hold for gaining access comprise the remainder of the table. Only the assenting positions (e.g., the resource is an important tool for gaining access) are reported, and the negative responses make up the balance in each cell.

In interpreting the figures at the top of the table, notice the advantage of for-profit organizations. Their poorest showing, 83.3 percent of above average staff, exceeds by nearly 10 percentage points the best performance among other types of groups. By these measures the nonprofits are also high-achievers. Well over two-thirds of their numbers report average or above average complements of money and staff, 74.1 percent in each instance. Not surprisingly, the citizen groups fare well in terms of their access to members with 64.6 percent of groups meeting the median and above threshold.[18] Their shortcomings are pronounced, however, with sizable gaps between their shares of above average staff and budgets and those of their competitors from other group categories.

Next let us review the way the advocates from disparate organizational settings describe what is valuable to them in securing access. The table includes some noteworthy similarities. Having an affiliate PAC, for example, is valued by private sector organizations to much the same

TABLE 4.1. Importance of Resources in Gaining Access, by Organization Type (in percentages)

	For-Profit	Nonprofit	Citizen	Administration
Organizational resources				
budget[a]				
≥ 2,000,000	100.0	74.1	46.4	n.a.
staff[a]				
≥ 35	83.3	74.1	32.1	n.a.
membership[a]				
≥ 7,000	91.7	51.9	64.6	n.a.
percentage in sample[a]	17.9	40.3	41.8	n.a.
credibility[b]	6.7	51.9	21.4	3.8
membership[b]	0.0	77.8	22.2	0.0
PAC affiliate[b]	20.0	22.2	25.0	0.0
Personal resources				
credibility[b]	40.0	18.5	25.0	23.1
issue expertise[b]	40.0	55.6	60.7	23.1
former congressional employee[b]	26.7	37.0	17.9	26.9
professional service[b]	40.0	44.4	35.7	15.4
position[b]	20.0	18.5	7.1	53.8
percentage in sample[b]	15.6	28.1	29.2	27.1

[a]*Source:* Ruffner 1988 and *Public Interest Profiles* 1988 ($N = 68$).

[b]*Source:* Interview responses to the question: "In reflecting on these and other assets (list provided), what ones do you consider to be important in explaining your access to the leaders you just identified?" ($N = 96$).

degree, anywhere from 20.0 to 25.0 percent. Of greater merit are two non-monetary assets—issue expertise and professional service. Agreement over their usefulness in gaining access is modest to high across the board, anywhere from 35.7 to 60.7 percent.

There are two dissimilarities of interest as well. First, the lobbyists from nonprofit organizations attest to possessing the widest array of useful assets. Notice in the column labeled *Nonprofit,* for example, that on five of the eight listed resources, anywhere from 37.0 to 77.8 percent of participants concur on the value of the asset. For-profit and citizen-based representatives by contrast show such agreement on only two or three assets.

Second, there is a remarkable lack of correspondence among what advocates value across organizational types. What large shares of respondents from nonprofits consider useful, membership (77.8 percent) and organizational credibility (51.9 percent), lobbyists from for-profits almost disdain. Instead the latter participants concur the most on the value of their own credibility (40 percent) and their knowledge of the issues (40 percent). Last by way of comparison, only lobbyists for the administration rate their institutional positions as the best resource for accessing House leaders. While to a lesser degree, they see the desirability of three assets that their nonadministrative counterparts also value—personal credibility, issue expertise, and former career ties to Congress.

From a practical standpoint these patterns make a lot of sense. The advocates stress the assets that they have in ample supply. Advocates from the AFL-CIO, the National Association of Manufacturers, and the National Association of Governors give primary credit for their access to the size and credibility of the organizations they represent. Advocates from corporations, which lack a volunteer base, such as American Express and BankBoston explain their access in terms of their own personal resources. This frees them to boast of something within their control—their trustworthiness and reputation for hard work. A twelve-year veteran from a large public relations firm who represented Mexico in the omnibus trade bill describes the importance of being a straight shooter: "It's hard to break through initially. . . . I do have a good reputation among many people, and some of my best allies are on the Hill. . . . The members have to trust you. You have to be a straight shooter" (interview, June 21, 1991). This person and other advocates from for-profit organizations, in particular, must talk their way into many Hill offices unassisted by the benefit of personal constituent connections. This is particularly true when corporate offices are concentrated in certain regions of the country, limiting any economic fallout to one or two congressional districts at best. In such circumstances, the advocates are forced to rely on their own competence and reputations for hard work. By their accounts it is personal credibility that serves them well.

In keeping with this rendering of events, the advocates from large occupational associations, which have members in every district, cite their organizations' size and credibility more than their own personal credibility when explaining their access to House leaders. A spokesperson for a large trade association explains being wooed by members of Congress because of the credibility that his organization's support brings to an issue.

> The National Association of Manufacturers is the voice of industry. We are a horizontal, very broad-based organization, and members of Congress are interested in working with us. In fact, sometimes congressmen reach out and ask us for support. . . . Members will justify their votes based on the fact that business supports the issue. In some cases it's like a competition where members from different sides of the debate are wooing us. (Interview, June 24, 1992)

Some citizen groups with large memberships explain their access on the basis of organizational credibility more than personal credibility. A spokesperson for the National Council of Churches put it this way: "The group represents 44 million constituents. These numbers give us the credibility that makes it next to impossible for any member to shut the door in our face" (interview, April 16, 1991).

Even more common (60.7 percent) among citizen groups is the explanation that the advocates' knowledge of the issues is what opens doors for them.

> Information is always valuable to the members. It's amazing sometimes the things you can tell them that they are not familiar with. Outsiders provide a different perspective and a useful perspective. We can be their eyes and ears. (Interview, February 4, 1992)

> They take cues from us. . . . They know we work the issue in a sincere way in the Senate as well as in the House. They get better overall information from us. The House talks to us about the Senate; the Senate talks to us about the House. (Interview, July 19, 1992)

By all accounts, experience with the issues and familiarity with the players, however accumulated, are valuable commodities on Capitol Hill. While fewer congressional alumni (17.9 percent) migrate to citizen-based interest groups than do lobbyists from occupational organizations (37.0 percent), the cause-oriented advocates sense no particular disadvantage when it comes to gaining access. By their accounts, one does not have to be a former employee or officeholder in the House to develop rapport and trust with members of Congress. These advocates, who have spent their entire careers in the private sector, credit their access in large part to the close bonds that have developed between them and their champions from one policy venture to the next.

The high percentage of *Position* in the administration column confirms that presidential appointees and bureaucrats use their formal position in the executive branch of government to access congressional leaders.

Do Variations in Organizational Resources Translate into Substantially Different Combinations of Leaders?

To answer this question, I examine for patterns between the personal and organizational resources on which advocates rely for gaining access and the compositions of the leadership networks they assemble.

Starting with the secondary data on budget, staff size, and membership, table 4.2 offers notably few differences on which to remark. Regardless of the size of their budgets, interest groups link up with approximately 12 leaders; 65 percent or so of these leaders are officeholders, and 80 percent of that group are Democrats. Nor are there great differences based on membership. Whether groups have above- or below-average shares of members seems to have little bearing on the size and construction of the networks. Indeed the only connection about which we can be somewhat confident, due to the statistical unlikelihood of its occurring (probability < .05), is the one between staff resources and the proportion of individuals on the leadership team that is Democratic, the majority party at the time. Organizations with above average levels of personnel reach out to fewer Democrats than do organizations with below average staffs, mean percents of 76 and 84, respectively. I will offer an interpretation of the staff connection subsequently. The point for emphasis here is that finding little correspondence between leadership selection and these institutional resources is informative. The data help confront the widespread belief that access depends on money and what money can buy.

Because lobbyists arguably act not on published accounts of institutional wealth and scarcity but on what they *perceive to be relevant* to the leaders with whom they desire access, the data in the remainder of table 4.2 is of particular interest. Once again, it is as enlightening to find no relationship when one is expected just as it is important to find something new and unexpected. Is it not remarkable, for example, that the only items to show no stable effect on leadership selection are the two that political pundits love to emphasize—campaign finance and the old boys network. Having a PAC affiliate through whom lobbyists can channel money and win indebtedness with choice leaders occurs, as does having a work history and old ties in Congress (table 4.1). With or without these resources, however, lobbyists rely on remarkably similar House leaders.

What do the advocates value that corresponds with variations in their leadership networks? Four assets, two organizational and two personal, are sufficiently stable to warrant discussion. Advocates who cite their organizations' credibility as a key to access reach out to more leaders than their complement. While the numerical difference is small, 13.8 represents a 27 percent increase over 10.8. The asset has no bearing on other aspects of the leadership team. The second organizational factor, perceived membership, has an effect that actual membership does not. I interpret this to mean that not all advocates rely on the resource to the same degree. Those who place importance on their membership base include more officeholders in their networks than those who disregard the resource or do not have it, mean percents of 84 and 63, respectively.

To explain this pattern, consider the special connection that constituents have with their representatives and the officeholders' ever-present concern over reelection. It makes sense that advocates in a position to do so would bypass congressional staff and work directly with officeholders. After all, the interest group members-as-voters have official relationships with the legislators. They have no such relationship with staff. And in cultivating their leadership contacts the advocates who perceive this advantage include in their leadership teams a greater proportion of officeholders than staff.

Last, I expect that one phenomenon is common to the patterns we see between leadership selection and two personal resources—credibility and professional service. Staff are the gatekeepers in Congress. As they screen calls and information, they witness firsthand the arguments and the professional service, when rendered, of the advocates. Positive day-to-day exposure builds credibility with staff, no doubt, more than with officeholders. When advocates subsequently look for champions on whom they can rely, it is eminently reasonable that they would approach the staff members with whom they have worked and with whom they have cultivated some mutual trust. The behavioral consequence of relying on personal credibility, then, is to reach out to 11 percent more staffers (or fewer officeholders) when assembling a Hill network. The connection between professional service and greater reliance on Democrats may also result from the fact that Democrats, ranking on all the committees and subcommittees at the time, had one-third again as many staff as their Republican

TABLE 4.2. Mean Percentage of Three Types of Issue Leaders, Accessed by Advocates' Organizational and Personal Resources

	Mean Number of Leaders Cited	Mean Percentage of Officeholders[c]	Mean Percentage of Democrats[d]	Mean Percentage of Party Leaders
Organizational resources				
budget[a]				
< 2,000,000	12.4	66	81	14
≥ 2,000,000	12.2	64	78	10
staff[a]				
< 35	11.5	65	84	13
≥ 35	12.9	65	76*	10
membership[a]				
< 7,000	11.3	58	82	11
≥ 7,000	12.8	68	77	11
credibility[b]				
no (74)	10.8	68	72	13
yes (22)	13.8*	72	74	9
membership[b]				
no (67)	12.2	63	81	12
yes (23)	11.8	84*	73	8
PAC affiliate[b]				
no (80)	11.7	69	73	13
yes (16)	13.9	68	75	9
Personal resources				
credibility[b]				
no (72)	11.8	72	72	13
yes (24)	10.8	61*	77	9
issue experience[b]				
no (52)	10.3	68	71	13
yes (44)	13.0*	70	76	11
worked in Congress[b]				
no (70)	11.2	69	73	13
yes (26)	12.7	70	73	9
professional service to leaders[b]				
no (62)	10.9	69	70	14
yes (32)	12.9	70	80*	10

[a]*Source:* Ruffner and *Public Interest Profiles* 1988 ($N = 65$).

[b]*Source:* Interview responses to the question: "In reflecting on these and other assets (list provided), what ones do you consider to be important in explaining your access to the leaders you just identified?" ($N = 96$).

[c]References to staff issue leaders plus officeholders sum to 100 percent.

[d]References to Democrats plus Republicans sum to 100. Only in this column is the denominator restricted to exclude staff.

* $p < .05$ in one-tailed test; ** $p < .01$ in two-tailed test.

counterparts. Thus advocates who use professional service as an inroad to the House leadership rely more heavily on the party in formal possession of the perks of office, including a disproportionate share of staff.

Having examined the connection between resources and organizations and resources and networks, we now examine the connections between organization types and networks.

Are There Patterns Between the Classifications of Advocacy Groups and the Assembly of Leaders They Access?

To address this question, I start with the big picture, first observing the ways in which groups tend to be similar. Then I review the disparities in organizational behavior and speculate on their origins given what we know about the politics of Congress, the executive branch of government, and interest groups.

Table 4.3 includes a few additional categories of individuals (members of pertinent standing committees and subcommittees and members of the powerful Rules Committee) as components of the leadership networks. Included as well (in the bottom half of the table) is a breakdown of the mean proportion of staffers who are pursued from different work settings within the chamber.

A cursory examination of the data reveals that all advocacy groups construct diverse leadership networks. On average, they go to many more officeholders than aides (at roughly a three-to-one ratio). When they enlist officeholders, they select far more majority-party members than minority-party members (at roughly a three-to-one ratio). Also, in almost every case (citizen groups excepted), advocates pursue in decreasing proportions officeholders who operate from the following positions: (1) full committees to which a bill is referred, (2) subcommittees to which a bill is referred, (3) party leadership offices, and (4) the House Rules Committee.

This comment on the value of committee membership expresses the sentiment of most lobbyists. "You really need experts and the committee people are seen as the experts. These are the people who rally the troops" (interview, July 8, 1991). The lobbyists give two explanations for eschewing the help of party leaders and members from Rules. For practical reasons they do not want to use up precious access over minor conflicts or over serious and unwinable ones. For strategic reasons, they often defer the task of meeting with these officials and those on the Rules Committee to their elected allies, who can speak with them as fellow members of the institution. Thus, when advocates contact party leaders for the purpose of promoting (or derailing) a bill, these contacts represent a small proportion of their overall Hill networks.

Because staffers operate from different bases of power, no parallels exist. However, more committee staffers than personal office staffers are included in the leadership networks across the board. Moreover, a high proportion of leadership networks (from 66 to 77 percent) reflect the joint efforts of legislative bosses and aides who work together in what Robert A. Salisbury and Kenneth A. Shepsle (1981) call congressional "enterprises." The percentage of aides who are named in tandem with an elected boss is actually far higher (96 percent), and the percent of officeholders who are cited with one or more of their aides (33 percent) is much lower.

To this point it appears that the advocates, regardless of their organizational sponsors, behave as if they used the same decision criteria to construct their leadership networks. And their propensity to favor Democrats and officeholders, as commonsensical as it seems, provides some important insights. In the first case, the skew toward selecting leaders from the majority party reaffirms some facts about the nature of influence and party politics in the House. In the second case, the tendency to identify officeholders over aides and enterprises over solo performers contributes new evidence to the unsettled debate over the role of staff in an institution that was designed to empower decision makers from one common pool—elected representatives of the people.

Tackling the party issue first, it makes sense in a struggle for power

TABLE 4.3.   Mean Percentage of Leaders Pursued by Organization Type

	For-Profit	Private Nonprofit	Citizen	Public Administration
Officeholders	71	75	70	80
majority party	75	76	85	58
full committees	79	72	15	54
subcommittees	47	43	10	30
party leadership	13	10	28	18
rules committee	1	6	18	0
Staff	29	25	30	20
majority party	45	40	61	42
full committee	16	16	13	36
subcommittee	31	27	6	16
personal office	14	11	17	12
party leadership office	0	8	35	0
enterprise	77	67	69	66

Note: Percentages do not sum to 100 because each House leader fits a number of categories. A reference to Rep. David E. Bonior (D-Michigan), for example, counts in calculating the proportion of Democrats as well as the proportion of party leaders (chief deputy whip). *Enterprise* captures the notion that staffers work hand in hand with their elected bosses (Salisbury and Shepsle 1981). The staffers in this category are cited along with their elected bosses.

that advocates would seek out the issue champions with the built-in procedural advantage of their numerical majority. For the past 40 years (ending with the 1994 congressional elections), House Democrats held this distinction. In congressional committees, through which almost all major legislation flows, it was the Democrats who held the exclusive agenda-setting prerogatives. And for more than a decade leading up to and including the study period, the Democrats used House rules to award themselves almost twice the number of committee staff that they granted their Republican counterparts. Through the powers of the majority leader and the Rules Committee, the majority party also controlled the timing of floor votes and the parameters of the debates. Under the circumstances, it stands to reason that advocates who are in the business of promoting certain desirable outcomes would pack their Hill networks with decidedly more Democrats than Republicans. Yet as the evidence also reveals, advocates rarely put all their eggs in the majority-party basket. Why is that?

I can think of two phenomena that explain the advocates' persistence in including some Republicans in their networks. First, many issues do not divide the chamber along party lines. When that occurs, leadership is undoubtedly shared, and the bipartisanship is reflected in the advocates' leadership networks. Second, accommodation is a strong norm among congressional leaders. We have seen that leaders build allegiances (within their party and across party lines) through attentive service and tolerant management styles. The practice of accommodation empowers individuals who would otherwise not have a voice in the policy-making process. Accommodation helps explain the level of leadership exhibited among minority-party members and nonranking members of both political parties. Because more disagreements over policy are characterized by a collegial style of shared leadership than manipulative one-upmanship, advocates see the wisdom in reaching out to leaders from both sides of the aisle and leaders up and down the committee system.

Similarly, for several reasons it makes sense for advocates to identify officeholders more than aides and to couple the identification of aides as leaders with the names of the patrons who hire them. For one thing, modern problems are too numerous and too complex for officeholders to champion without the assistance of talented, committed staff. Moreover, many professional staff, particularly those from congressional committees, devote full attention to policy matters, whereas their principals must contend with the competing demands of the office and the daunting pressures to raise money for upcoming campaigns. Based on availability alone, staff are likely to get involved. Arguably, the more that officeholders delegate responsibilities to trusted aides, the more aggressive the officeholders can be about assuming the command of a larger swath of policy concerns.

While these data do not test the connection between staff size and one's leadership achievements, the large proportion of cited enterprises is consistent with my interpretation.

Next, the advocates enlighten us on a possible connection between staff competence and the leadership potential of officeholders and aides. From chapter 2 we know that staff members cannot browbeat their bosses into championing issues that do not interest them. According to the study participants, however, inexperienced and ill-informed staff can thwart officeholders from assuming commands that are in the officeholders' interest to accept. One comment illustrates the point made by several advocates: ["When seeking issue leaders] you look for staffers, who are knowledgeable on the issues and are capable of articulating and explaining issues very well [to their principals]" (interview, May 30, 1991). One responsibility that busy legislators commonly entrust with unelected staff is the filtering job that is needed to cope with the numerous demands that are part and parcel with the legislators' job (Fox and Hammond 1977, S. Patterson 1970). Apparently, advocates discriminate when they search for issue leaders and avoid officeholders who employ gatekeepers who are either unfamiliar with their bosses' agenda or are incapable of presenting the subtleties of the issues in a clear and compelling manner.

In my previous work on the partnerships that form between committee leaders and their *senior* aides, I find little evidence to suggest that officeholders are misguided by their subordinates. As the committee staff directors tell it, miscalculations in their gatekeeping function can lead to catastrophe (loss of office for the elected official and subsequent loss of a job for the aide). As a consequence, the aides quickly learn to discriminate between the policy challenges that fit their bosses' interests, and they interpret demands from outsiders with these tastes in mind (DeGregorio 1994, 1988).

In the current study, where leaders may be identified from obscure positions, often without the benefit of seasoned staff, the lobbyists' insight about staff competence is especially valuable. In the advocates' search for individuals to champion a cause, there is little room for congressional aides who, however well intentioned, misjudge their bosses' commitment to shepherding an issue. Officeholders who gain the recognition of others reportedly do so, in part at least, because they are sound managers of their own time and that of their employees.

Returning now to table 4.3, some disparities in behavior across group types warrant discussion. Of the four types of organizations, the citizen-based groups and the administration most frequently break rank. For example, the citizen groups access a higher proportion of Democrats (85 percent) and party leaders (28 percent) than any other groups. The administration accesses a higher proportion of officeholders (80 percent) and a lower proportion of Democrats, the majority party (58 percent), than any other groups. These partisan disparities can be explained on the basis of the ideological affinities between the leaders and the advocates. Citizen associations tend to be more liberal than business, trade, and professional associations. Citizen groups, finding many kindred spirits within the Democratic party, concentrate much more of their efforts within that party. For their part, administration officials were promoting the views of Republican President Ronald Reagan, the champion of the conservative agenda. To every extent possible these advocates also looked for ideologically compatible partners among their partisans in the House. However, given the prevailing circumstance of divided government, in which one party controls the White House and the other party controls the Congress, the president's lobbyists had no choice but to construct bipartisan networks. Under different conditions (when one party controls both branches of government), I would anticipate a stronger partisan flavor to executive-congressional relations.

Next, in the background section on administration officials, we considered two alternative depictions of their Hill networks. One held that status differences between career civil servants and presidential appointees would result in the two types of players selecting different sets of leaders (i.e., civil servants would secure access to higher numbers of aides, and appointees would secure access to higher numbers of officeholders). The second scenario held that civil servants and appointees would attract similar numbers of officeholders because they each had valuable insights to offer the congressional leaders. What appointees lacked in institutional memory and expertise they made up for in proximity to the president. What civil servants lacked in proximity they made up for in expertise and a familiarity with old battles won and lost. The high proportion of officeholders (80 percent) in the administration officials' networks, as revealed in table 4.3, persists even when the data are broken down by executive position. The fact that bureaucrats face no apparent barriers in accessing officeholders supports the second of the two scenarios—bureaucrats possess expertise and knowledge of past politics that compensate for any status differences in their positions relative to presidential appointees.

Returning the discussion to citizen groups' outreach to party leaders, first recall from table 4.2 that two organizational conditions were associated with higher shares of party leaders: a below-median budget and a below-median number of staff. These two factors return now in table 4.3 to play a part in the citizen groups' propensity to work with a high proportion of party leaders. Some of the groups in this cell are small and financially less well off. When they reach out to two or three members of the party hierarchy who constitute their entire networks, the average proportion of party leaders pursued by this category of groups increases accordingly.

Having examined what is similar and what is different about organizations' resources and their selection of leaders, we can now approach the question of promotional impact.

How Much Disparity Exists in the Advocates' Assessments of Their Policy Accomplishments?

The advocates were asked, "On a 100-point scale (with 100 being high), how close does the actual policy outcome resemble the one you were attempting to achieve?" Clearly this is as much a measure of the advocates' satisfaction as it is a measure of organizational influence. This is so because advocates who start out with low expectations of what they can achieve are likely to perceive a smaller gap between actual and idealized outcomes than if they had sky-high expectations at the outset and failed in their attempts to reconcile the difference. Moreover, the groups that promote a policy that is similar to the outcome may not have influenced the outcome at all. Rather, they may simply have tastes for policy that are remarkably similar to those of the House leaders who were victorious in the end. With these limitations noted, it is important nonetheless to consider the advocates' impressions of events and learn what we can from their experiences.

Also, the aggregate figures on what advocates received for their efforts tell us something about the legislators' capacity for meeting the expectations of a highly vocal and discordant class of petitioners. Taking this last point first, the evidence clearly reaffirms that the House is a very responsive institution. Only six participants, roughly 7 percent of the 81 individuals who answered this question, reported that they got nothing for their efforts. More than 10 percent of the advocates reported obtaining everything they wanted, and a full 50 percent of the sample reported receiving 70 percent or more of what they were attempting to achieve.

I link this high rate of satisfaction to the coequal nature of the officeholders and the personal manner in which influence is applied. We know that coalition formation entails a seemingly endless amount of horse-trading, for which the institution is commonly derided as unconscionably slow and aimless. Yet when leaders look for policy trade-offs that will win over new support, while being careful not to undermine existing support, what are they doing but accommodating greater and greater numbers of people—elected officials and the citizens and groups they represent?

Not until we break down the responses by organization type do important disparities emerge in the way the advocates assess their accomplishments. The two groups with the lowest percentages (17.1 in each case) of above-average scores are the for-profits and the administration. The nonprofit occupational groups have the highest percent (37.1) of above-average scores, and the citizen groups take second place, with 28.6 percent above-average scores.

What accounts for these results? Two possibilities are easily tested. First, the difference in satisfaction is attributable to differences in the advocates' expectations: Those who support the bill "as is" ($N = 25$) should report higher satisfaction with their achievements than advocates who promote change ($N = 56$), either strengthening or weakening the legislation. When the advocates' scores are grouped in this way, however, no statistical difference in satisfaction appears. The second possibility is that the advocates' reported accomplishments are linked to the initiatives themselves and the amount of change they undergo as legislators attempt to accommodate competing views. To test this line of reasoning we compare the mean scores of two groups of advocates, those who participated in the debates over Contra aid and the nuclear test ban ($N = 33$), the issues in which there is little appreciable change from initiation to passage, and everyone else ($N = 48$). Here, as well, the results are unremarkable.

A third explanation, while somewhat beyond the scope of this inquiry, is also worthy of thorough consideration. Here I am speaking of the fact that the two categories of groups to claim the fewest rewards for their labors (for-profits and the administration) are the only groups of the set whose institutional maintenance is not inextricably connected to the commitments of volunteer members—their money, political connections, energies, and time.

The shareholders of a corporation, for example, make investment decisions on the basis of financial statements about the companies' profitability, not on the basis of who wins what battles in Congress. While it is true that being on the losing side of a policy fight may partly account for the investors' woes, there are ample guilty parties to blame before reproaching the organizations' lobbyists. Fluctuations in the market and management decisions come immediately to mind.

Presidential appointees and bureaucrats comprise the other class of advocates to admit having sizable gaps between what they wanted and what they achieved. Not being in the business of wooing volunteers or seeking political and financial patronage from their accomplishments on Capitol Hill, these lobbyists, like their corporate counterparts, are free to criticize their own efficacy with little fear of inflicting damage on the people and the institutions they represent. Indeed, these individuals, in particular the political appointees who are accustomed to making public pronouncements about their bosses' performance, could find it profitable to accentuate the difficulties they face in battling the opposition party at the other end of Pennsylvania Avenue. Such admissions are so commonplace, in fact, that it is tempting to surmise that the administration officials deliberately use the approach to arouse the attention and sympathy of their supporters across the country.

If advocates' interpretations of their policy accomplishments are as entangled with their goals for institutional maintenance as these two scenarios depict, we see that the advocates who are most at risk of downplaying their losses are those from the nonprofits and the citizen-based, cause-oriented groups who must guard their organizations' reputations as participants of consequence. That the advocates' assessments of their achievements conform to this explanation of their behavior does not make it so. The pattern is nonetheless suggestive and warrants further tests of the connection between perceived accomplishments and institutional pressures for self-maintenance through membership recruitment.

Two types of data are required to determine the extent to which advocates' institutional incentives inadvertently bias upward or downward the true picture of who wins and who loses in these high-stakes policy skirmishes. First, we need the subjective accounts of the participants themselves. Only they know what they were attempting to accomplish, and if the participants of this study are a good guide, their sponsors launch promotional campaigns for a variety of reasons. The groups succeed in some areas and fail in others, at one and the same time. Asking them to measure their accomplishments on one policy dimension, as I do here, is problematic. The 20 percent abstention rate on this question and the advocates' near universal tendency to qualify their achievement scores attest to the difficulty.

Second, to complement the advocates' accounts of their organizations' policy aims and accomplishments, we need some independent measures of what was achieved. This could entail, for example, information from the public record (e.g., briefing documents and hearing testimony) that permits a comparison of what different groups called for in the legislation and what the lawmakers agreed to at different junctures in the course of deliberation. It seems to me that neither account alone will capture the complexity of the situation and the interactive nature of the process.

Summary and Conclusion

This chapter operates under the assumption that leaders and advocates need each other to pass legislation of any consequence. The advocates need accommodating leaders to interject their points into the formal decision-making process. And the legislators need information, brokers, and confidants to help them assemble enough votes for passage. Because the elected officials are the only ones with the formal legitimacy to introduce and champion issues, they become the dominant partners in these mutually satisfying relationships.

It is important to note that the qualitative stories about what opens doors on Capitol Hill comport well with the respondents' more formalized assessments. In general, credibility (sometimes personal and sometimes institutional), experience advocating on prior issues, the provision of in-kind professional service, and a work history in Congress appear with greater frequency than does campaign involvement or the size and diffusion of the membership base.

When these reports are broken down by organization type, some important discrepancies emerge. The personal and institutional attributes that take prominence for the four types of advocates differ profoundly from one organizational category to the next. For-profit representatives mention personal credibility and PAC affiliations with irregular frequency. Advocates from nonprofits mention a disproportionately high incidence of five characteristics—the size of their member base, the credibility of their institution, their knowledge of the issues, professional service, and former employment in Congress. For the citizen-based participants, it is their knowledge of the issues, their professional service, and their PAC affiliations that receive pronounced mention. And for the administration officials, more often than not it is their position in the bureaucracy that opens doors on Capitol Hill. What is interesting about this accounting is that in every case there is a personal and organizational nature to the respondents' explanations of their access, and different organizations stress different combinations of resources.

Perhaps it is the advocates' ingenuity and their diverse resources that explain the remarkable similarity we see when we compare the size and the composition of the leadership networks across group types. With few exceptions, lobbyists, regardless of sponsor and auspice, reach out to incredibly similar combinations of leaders: officeholders more than aides, majority partisans more than minority partisans, full committee members more than subcommittee members, and Rules Committee and formal party leaders in smallest number.

The two organization types that behave most at odds with overall averages are the citizen-based groups, who enlist a disproportionate number of formal party leaders, and administration officials, who work with an uncommonly large number of officeholders, minority-party officeholders at that. Nonprofit and for-profit entities, both with an occupational focus, secure access with quite similar types of leaders.

In this whole picture there are decidedly more similarities than differences. So it is with our look into the advocates' satisfaction with their efforts to shape policy according to their own tastes. In particular, very few organizations report that they get nothing for their efforts, and the disappointments that do exist occur among the most amply endowed (for-profits) and well-connected (administration officials) entities. But to emphasize this result obscures one that is equally germane. Most advocates, regardless of their organizational affiliation, are pleased with the policy outcomes the institution produces.

CHAPTER 5

Practical Tips and Theoretical Guideposts

The preceding chapters report what professional advocates observed as they searched for individuals in the U.S. House of Representatives to take up the lead on six specific policies the advocates cared deeply about. In this chapter I first assemble several practical rules of thumb that are instructive for lobbyists and policymakers alike, whatever their policy challenges. The insights come from lengthy conversations with the study participants as they reflected on their years, sometimes entire careers, of being on the lookout for and cultivating profitable relationships with choice leaders.

For readers with a taste for unraveling the puzzles that politics presents us, I subsequently reflect on the way the results of this inquiry guide further research and learning. This theoretical appraisal follows a discussion of the continuities and changes that have occurred in the House since the late 1980s. The update on recent events helps justify using the findings as I suggest, for it substantiates the stability that exists in several conditions found here to be important in shaping leadership and access in Congress. They include institutional rules and structures, the personal ambitions and talents of the policymakers, and the political context in which the action occurs.

The book ends as it began, with a return to three criticisms that shadow the U.S. Congress. I review the evidence and evaluate each claim with the new insights supplied by this investigation.

Implications for Practice

Beyond describing the particular features about the champions of the six policies under investigation, the advocates offered several rules of thumb that may be applied by others who engage in the business of promotional politics. Four themes emerge from the advocates' qualitative accounts of their day-to-day work with congressional leaders.[1] Call them the *A, B, C, D*'s of congressional networking: *A*ssess the situation; *B*e patient and persistent; *C*onform to the flow of events; and *D*on't put all your eggs in one leadership basket. Using excerpts from the interview transcripts, I will discuss these in turn.

The Voices of the Experts: The Do's and Don'ts
of Congressional Networking

Assess the situation. To secure an audience with officials who have the capacity to move policies through the institution, advocates first assess what they and their organizations can bring to the conflict. As in any other partnership where mutual gains take place from an exchange of goods, moreover, assessments are made by both parties to the deal. In the words of one lobbyist, "Basically, the matter of access to members is a meeting of the minds. The interest groups ask, 'Who can we get to be a leader?' and the members of Congress ask, 'How can you help us if we take on this issue?' When that happens simultaneously, people look to each other and decide that it's a good fit" (citizen group member, June 13, 1991). What is called for is a mutual and open assessment of the partners' assets.

> You talk with your champions candidly. . . . It's a team approach. The champion is the captain of the team. You talk about whose votes are needed and who can deliver. You share assets and liabilities honestly. If your strategy for success relies on so-and-so to deliver and that's just boasting, you've lost the vote. You need to know who is going to deliver and who won't, and you need to know this when you determine your strategy. (Governmental association advocate, September 13, 1991)

The advocates, furthermore, know to accept the political realities about their champions and not ask them to do something that goes against the leaders' interests: "We have a good strategic sense. We don't ask them to do what they can't do. . . . We will not attack them for not being perfect. We will applaud them for doing what is feasible. This is one way of continuing rapport in gaining access" (occupational nonprofit member, July 19, 1992). One participant commented on the triangular nature of the give-and-take: "Congressmen have 28 balls up in the air at any one time. Government advocates have many as well. Both individuals get information from different sources and share it. We [lobbyists] take tips from them about who else to reach out to along the way and they take tips from us" (law firm member, June 28, 1991).

When it comes to explaining what attracts the partners to one another, the stories are varied. Two perspectives follow.

> We're a research organization. Information is all we have. We don't have any grass roots connections. However, we have a reputation for being thoughtful and up-front. Congressmen, particularly [David]

Bonior in the case of Contra aid, sought me out because I went to the region so often and had information on breaking events having to do with negotiations. (Washington think tank advocate, May 30, 1992)

We represent state human service commissioners. They are part of the governors' cabinets, [the governors] who, in turn, have enormous credibility with members of Congress. Credibility, that's our engine. (Governmental association advocate, September 13, 1991)

These accounts amplify what is generally apparent in one interview after another. Lobbyists from member-based organizations emphasize the credibility they receive from their constituent networks. Those from organizations with no members to boast of rely on the appeal of their information and their personal credibility.

Also, the advocates discriminate when they search for individuals to shepherd the issues they care about. One participant's straightforward assessment of several individuals with whom he worked when championing test ban legislation is typical of the process.

Markey had a big mouth, at times, and pissed off some of the senior members. He's learned to tone it down a little bit, and he's gained some skills since then, but at the time he was very hard working and commanded respect. Downey was terrific at building coalitions with the leadership. He was a great reconciler. Schroeder sticks with things, and she's a powerful speaker. One of too few women in the House, she's sort of a freelancer. More than anyone else in the [leadership] group she really didn't work with the team the way the others did. Gephardt is a terrific coalition builder. He listens to people. Sabo, I respect him enormously. Barney Frank has a reputation as being the most articulate, second only to the Speaker of the House. He's funny, and he's also hard to work with. But he does what he says. Russo's a Chicago tough-guy type. He doesn't care who he pisses off. He wasn't particularly an expert on the testing issue, but he was passionate about the budget—defense versus domestic. He had a position on the Budget Committee, and he worked at that issue very well. (Citizen group advocate, June 14, 1991)

The lesson is: discriminate. Advocates choose to work with certain individuals in Congress because they bring something special to the process. Advocates do not reach out willy-nilly to anyone with whom they can get access. Because they are selective about whom they work with, furthermore, they offered advice on what it takes to open doors on Capitol Hill.

Be patient and persistent. Whether fee-for-service consultants from high-dollar public relations firms or low-paid staff from fledgling citizen-based groups, most advocates concur: Not only must they be expert in arriving at convincing explanations for why a busy House leader would want to invest a few moments with them, the advocates also must be prepared to confine their requests for time to brief encounters that show promise of mutual gain and, once that is established, ask persistently for an audience and be prepared to wait. Here is a sampling of their accounts.

> Members of Congress are very busy, and a smart lobbyist will make their visits quick. Scheduling secretaries pay attention to this. Next time you go back and ask for a meeting, they like you because you kept to your word about being very brief. (Labor union lobbyist, July 8, 1991)

> We were relentless. We went back several times. You can't just go to these folks once. You have to be committed enough to go back and talk with them on successive occasions. (Governmental association advocate, June 13, 1991)

> The halls of Congress are remarkably open. . . . You keep knocking. It's a process, not a one-time thing. (Citizen group advocate, June 12, 1991)

Beyond universal agreement on the need for persistence, the study participants largely concur that leaders change and multiply over the course of the policy debate.

Conform to the flow of events. As they describe it, the advocates start where the action is and add leaders along the way. Few advocates exchange leaders from one vantage point (subcommittees) for leaders from another vantage point (full subcommittees). Rather, they maintain their contacts and work with more individuals as time elapses. In their own words, the process goes like this.

> The stage that legislation is in definitely shapes who we approach and what we do. When you want to help shape the language of a bill or committee report, you go to the subcommittee people. You talk to staff, maybe the chair. Maybe you get [invited as] a witness at a hearing. As it moves to the full committee there's different staff; sometimes you need to check in with them, find out where the full committee chair stands, work with them. [Members of the] Rules Committee

can be a crucial. They are trying to create a friendly or a hostile set of rules by which the issue is debated and voted. At the floor level we contact swing voters. You may need people to make a floor speech. Not all issues are the same. On some issues you know in advance who the swings are going to be because there has been a long history of votes on the issue. On some other issues its a complete mystery. (Church group advocate, June 5, 1991)

You start with a small nucleus and just build and build. You anticipate who you are going to need for the floor, who's going to be useful from the Rules Committee and the Appropriations Committee. (Law firm lobbyist, June 21, 1991)

What you do is build as you go. You try not to drop anybody off the coalition but basically build throughout. And you try to get ready for a floor fight. I mean, you'd like to avoid the floor fight, but you're always getting ready for it. (Labor union lobbyist, July 8, 1991)

Different talents are needed along the way. Advocates recognize this and look for individuals with agenda-setting privileges early and eloquence late in the lawmaking cycle.

Almost everyone agrees that it helps to establish close working relationships with an array of leaders who bring to the fight different talents, perspectives, and privileges with which to woo, cajole, and bully their way to success. What follows is some Capitol Hill wisdom on which there is some difference of opinion.

Don't put all your eggs in one leadership basket. The experts agree that some combination of commitment, clout, and expertise is needed on the leadership team. What the experts do not always see eye-to-eye on is their means for discerning these qualities. Based on their personal experiences, spanning as many as 30 years in the business, this is what the experts have to say about finding leaders in Congress.

You want someone who knows and cares about the issue, someone with leadership and or seniority. Solarz is an example, as is Moakley. Solarz went way out on a limb to support the president on the Persian Gulf. He was able to do that because he had long experience on foreign affairs, and people looked to him for cues. In the case of Moakley, he had no experience, but he suddenly became real vocal. As chairman of the Rules Committee, people started to pay attention to his positions. . . . This sort of recognition and reputation with the press applies less with members of the Senate. Reputation and longevity are particularly important in the House because there are many people who never gain the attention of the press. It's reserved for a few. In the Senate, there are many people who have that sort of recognition, and they can be a player without the longevity and the expertise. In the House, I'd say it takes being chairman of a committee, active on the issue, having a reputation and longevity. (Citizen group advocate, June 6, 1991)

First and most important, you need a leader who is willing to do the work, the inside work. We can do the outside work. But [only] members talk to members and the [party] leadership. The second thing is finding leaders who are not controversial or pegged on a particular extreme. You want to have a spectrum of ideologies working on an issue and a spectrum of regions, although on this issue [test ban] it [regional cooperation] was not possible. (Citizen group advocate, June 24, 1991)

Many lobbyists conclude that commitment and committee position go hand in hand. As a consequence, they recommend starting the search for a leader in issue-relevant committees.

On labor issues, I go to Bartlett. He's connected to the right committee. He's eloquent. He has passion, and as he goes so does one hundred or so other votes. Translating this into the general case, I would include: committee position, keen interest, and expertise. (Governmental association advocate, August 6, 1991)

First you cut out the junior Republicans, then you find the committee link and go to senior Republicans and Democrats on the relevant committees. I work in a bipartisan fashion because with divided government you must. You can't ignore either of the two parties in the Congress. (Law firm lobbyist, June 21, 1991)

Committee assignments also serve as a good rule of thumb in locating leaders with the political legitimacy and specialized knowledge to intervene.

Understanding the issue is the most important thing, and you need someone who is politically positioned to work it. It's not necessary that they are the most senior person; Matsui as an example. . . . Having served on the Telecommunications Subcommittee on Energy and

Commerce before coming to Ways and Means, he spoke with authority and expertise. People looked to him for information. He also had the presence of a political leader. It's partially personality. As in any organization, a lot of human dynamics are involved. Some people are viewed as leaders and others are not, and Matsui has the chemistry on both of these dynamics, knowing the issue and being politically positioned and being seen as a potential leader within the Democratic party. (Law firm lobbyist, June 28, 1991)

According to a smaller number of advocates, committees provide too fine a screen for policy champions.

[Being] knowledgeable on the issue, having their heart in the issue, [and having] clout is always helpful. You look to allies, hopefully, on substantive committees, but they're not always there. (Citizen group advocate, June 7, 1991)

Ideological commitment [is first]. For many Republicans, committee assignments are secondary. They're not in the majority; they don't have as many staffers, and they make their name in ways other than the committee connection. (Foreign government official, June 29, 1991)

I always check to see if the interest is a personal fancy of the member or if it is relevant to reelection. It is the latter commitment that will get you through thick and thin. (Citizen group advocate, April 5, 1991)

For a variety of reasons, people may have developed a range of contacts making them very good policy leaders. These are members who help other members get on the committees they want. Or members help other members with fund-raising, etc. It's not always obvious how these connections are made. (Presidential appointee, June 24, 1991)

This latter respondent is describing the favors that some members do for others, as a way of storing up chits, which can be recalled in time of need. Because only the parties to the deal keep score of who is indebted to whom, she considers this a "wild card" in the political process.

Personal commitment and knowledge of the issues are credentials that everyone associates with congressional leadership. Where the advocates diverge somewhat is in their experiences with locating leaders with these attributes. Committees provide a sound shortcut for most lobbyists.

A small number of advocates prefer to find leaders through the electoral connection. Find an affected district, and you will find a committed officeholder. Longevity, clout, and political know-how are helpful credentials if you find them, but these are not the first characteristics that advocates look for in a leader. Many experts, for example, eschew reaching out to the top echelons of the political parties. As they describe it, the advocates do not want to use up precious access over minor conflicts or over serious and unwinnable ones. Furthermore, the outsiders often defer the task of meeting with these officials and those on the Rules Committee to their elected allies, who can speak with them as fellow members of the institution. When advocates contact party leaders for the purpose of promoting (or derailing) a bill, these contacts invariably make up a tiny fraction of their overall Hill access.

Leadership, Access, and Advocacy: Then and Now

When change occurs in congressional politics, procedures, and policies, three ingredients are typically involved: (1) the tastes and ambitions of the members, (2) the structure (or rules of the game) that conditions behavior, and (3) the policy environments within which legislators operate. I consider each of these in turn.

The Membership: Officeholders and Aides

Since the days of the 100th Congress, much has changed and much remains the same in the House membership. For example, just 55 percent of the representatives in the 104th Congress served in 1988. When this figure is broken down by leadership recognition, the difference is not great between the departure rates of those named and not named as leaders: 46.3 percent and 43.8 percent, respectively. When one considers the proportion of prominent positions left open by departing officeholders, the implication for those wishful of wielding power is plain. In descending order of net change in personnel, the figures include party officers (71 percent), standing committee leaders (62 percent), party whips (45 percent), and subcommittee leaders (44 percent).

Balancing out this remarkable transfiguration are two practices that interject a degree of continuity in the institution. First is the norm of seniority. When individuals are sought to fill leadership positions, by rule and custom officeholders give advantage to those among them who have served a long time. A closely related pattern is the stability that exists in the committee system. After having waited the requisite number of years to qualify for a position of rank, committee leaders seldom retire their privileges. As a consequence of these two phenomena, individuals who were in office during the time of the study continued to dominate the scene in the 104th Congress. In descending order, the proportions of veteran officeholders in possession of prominent posts are: standing committee leaders (96 percent), party officers (95 percent), subcommittee leaders (89 percent), and whip posts (77 percent). Furthermore, more veterans of the 100th Congress gained than lost ground in the formal leadership hierarchies. For example, 62 percent of the representatives either added new privileges to their existing portfolios or gave up one position (e.g., subcommittee rank) for a more favored one (e.g., full committee rank). Thirty-three percent of the returning legislators achieved no change in rank, and 5 percent lost a leadership post they possessed in the late 1980s. Where the rookie legislators are most visible are in the whip offices and the subcommittees, where they represent 33 percent and 11 percent shares, respectively.

This blend of change and continuity is probably good for the country. The new blood within the top echelons of the institution will introduce fresh ideas and energy to cope with the policy challenges that lie ahead. The turnover within the rank-and-file House membership will interject into the debate many new demands and perspectives. Also, the stable forces that remain in both camps to recall old battles and prior deals will speed coalition building to some degree. However, the uncertainty that comes with change will surely offer opportunities for new individuals and groups to participate meaningfully in the formulation of future policies.

Perhaps the biggest change in membership is the one-third cutback in professional committee staff. Several outcomes can be anticipated as a consequence of the downsizing of personnel; however, none of the underlying behavioral trends picked up by these data seem threatened. Majority-party officeholders, still the recipients of the lion's share of staff, will continue to be advantaged over their minority-party colleagues. Minority-party staff members, who become issue leaders in their own right, are themselves so outflanked by their counterparts from the other side of the aisle that their recognition as policy movers will continue to be depressed. Furthermore, with all committees sharing the staff cutbacks as they do, we can expect no marked change in the committees' capacity to spawn leaders. Those that made excellent vantage points for gaining visibility and attracting followers before will continue to do so now. What the reductions in staff may trigger, interestingly, is the House members' dependence on outside advocates for helpful and timely information. With fewer aides to turn to, it is only natural that officeholders and aides in positions of steering policy will rely on their trusted contacts from the pressure group community, thereby perpetuating the conditions for the policy-making partnerships that these respondents describe.

Rules and Procedures

The House of the 104th Congress is different in many ways from the House of the 100th Congress. The most important procedural and structural changes include (1) three fewer standing committees; (2) the withdrawal of funds to support legislative service organizations (LSOs), the 28 caucuses that received money and space for mobilizing interest in the concerns of their members; (3) six- and eight-year limits on the consecutive years of service allowed committee leaders and the Speaker, respectively; (4) restrictions in the Speaker's prerogative to simultaneously refer bills to multiple committees (sequential referral is still allowed); (5) a ban on proxy voting in committees; (6) automatic roll call votes when taxing and spending issues come to the floor; and (7) a ban on closing committee meetings to the public except when the open forum would endanger national security, compromise sensitive information, or degrade or incriminate persons (Cloud 1995).

As with any organizational shift in policies that redistributes the rights and resources awarded its members, we can expect these procedural changes to advantage some leaders and advocates more than others in their attempts to promote legislation. At issue is the size of their anticipated impacts. I concur with David Cloud's (1995) assessment that, while patently important and worthy of attention, these reforms are not revolutionary. Rather, they fit a long tradition of rules changes that for decades have focused on (1) expanding opportunities for more officeholders to play meaningful roles in the lawmaking process, and (2) stimulating public awareness of what is taking place inside the institution. So while they may create perturbations in the flow of events, I expect no major upheaval to occur in the way leaders attract followers and the way advocates gain access.

Consider, for example, what will happen as a consequence of limiting the number of years ranked leaders may hold positions of authority within the chamber. The top committee slots will of necessity pass to more junior members of both parties. While the diffusion in power may depress the effect tenure has on leadership recognition (chap. 2), the old bulls who have retired their formal prerogatives will not just disappear from the scene. Rather, their accumulated knowledge of the issues and the old battles will ensure for them an important place at the negotiating table. The model of identifying leaders, as we do here, through their formal positions and their personal talents accommodates this type of reform.

Also, while the legislators modified some committee jurisdictions to allow for the elimination of three standing committees, nothing in the rules changes offsets the relative importance of committee assignments. The panels with broad jurisdictions and power over taxing and spending will continue to play a major role in launching leaders and attracting advocates, just as we have observed here.

Next, the media made a great deal of the cutback in funds to LSOs, yet I see no real change to leadership, access, and advocacy as a result of the policy. It is true that some individuals caught the attention of their fellows in the chamber because of their formal positions on prominent caucuses. In part, Charles Rangel was identified for chairing the Select Committee on Narcotics Abuse and Control, just as Patricia Schroeder gained some attention as the Cochair of the Congressional Caucus for Women's Issues (Richardson 1987). Explanations of leadership appeal on the basis of these positions, however, are infrequent. What really contributes to a leader's following in the House, according to the advocates, is the combination of committees one operates from. There is no substitute for being on two standing committees that have broad jurisdictions and active agendas. The cutback in support of LSOs, ironically, could free more members to devote more time to official committee business, and this is my interpretation of what really counts in gaining recognition for policy-making. Furthermore, advocates make no mentions of gaining access to important leaders through LSOs. By and large they seek access through committees that are empowered to formulate legislation (chap. 4), a responsibility that was never available to caucuses.

The new restriction on the Speaker's referral powers does not necessarily preclude several committees from participating in the early formulation of a bill, just as they did at the time of this study. It simply means that committees with overlapping jurisdictions will have to wait for a nod from the Speaker to begin their hearings. Elongating the lawmaking process in this way may slow down the assembly of leaders to some extent, yet do nothing to hamper the same individuals from participating meaningfully in the process.

The ban on proxy voting, the move to open committees to scrutiny, and the mandate for roll call votes formalize practices that were widely in use anyway. For the committee leaders who are directly affected by the first of these reforms, in particular, I expect they will adapt and use the restrictions to their advantage. They may choose to structure choice and call for votes when key adversaries are absent from committee rooms, or they may refrain from such coercive behavior and build a following through a more conciliatory management style. Whatever the approach taken, we can anticipate no change one way or the other when it comes to the power of committee chairs. Their authority is not threatened.

What is more, the real staying power of these changes and their effects on patterns of leadership and advocacy will depend on how long they endure. The next Congress may rewrite the rule book and do something revolutionary to threaten status quo power arrangements, but these revisions in the House rules do nothing of the sort.

Last, as important as the aforementioned changes in rules and procedures are to the balance of power within the institution, changes in the electoral process and the rewards of service are paramount. Elected officials construct chamber rules and resources (such as staff, the frank, and travel money) to suit their primary concern for reelection. Agreement over this or that policy solution comes only after individual representatives can see a way to explain their votes to the constituents who placed them in office. Until change occurs in campaign processes (e.g., finance reforms and term limits) that is of such a magnitude as to upset legislators' preoccupation with the parochial interests of their constituents, I expect little real change in the determinants of leadership and the processes of coalition building. Until such reforms occur, and they are unlikely to come from officeholders who secured office under status quo arrangements, the endeavor of channeling members of Congress to coalesce around common policy solutions will continue to resemble the herding of cats. More than formal authority, it will take wit, reason, and perspicacity.

The Policy Environment

The political agenda, according to Barbara Sinclair (1989, 51), is "the set of problems and policy proposals being seriously debated by the attentive public and by policy makers." The definition is apt because it acknowledges a place for the advocates, officeholders, and aides who are the focus of this work. No player may be extracted from the process, because each has a function in keeping issues alive. For ideas to reach the congressional agenda, they need to capture the interest and commitment of a critical mass of lawmakers and staff. To do this and survive the labyrinthine process of successive committee and floor reviews, policy initiatives require devoted advocates working outside the institution who keep their members and some portion of the mass public alert to the legislators' accomplishments. Who provides the first impetus in the process is almost impossible to know.[2] Experience and observation lead me to conclude, however, that it takes the sustained efforts of all three participants—the lawmakers, their staff members, and the advocates from the interest group community—to attain passage of major legislation.

This confluence of participation may be unnecessary when few citizens are touched by a policy and when broad cross sections of affected citizens agree on what the federal government should do. However, when Congress attempts to contain the deficit, lift children out of poverty, control violence, stem the flow of illegal drugs, clean up the environment, and instill the work ethic in new generations of Americans, it is engaging in an unparalleled level of social engineering. Battles over what government does to address these and other problems of this magnitude involve moral, economic, cultural, and philosophical questions about which honorable people disagree. Finding the solutions and amassing the support, whether it is to do something or to do nothing governmental to intervene, will require strong and capable leaders. What is more, the basic picture that is described here roughly approximates reality even as shifts occur in the party in control of the institutions. Some names change, but the general dynamics do not.

Technological advances in the media and polling industries open additional opportunities for change in the interest-group community. With the advent of fax machines and gavel-to-gavel coverage of congressional hearings and floor debates, for example, more newcomers may find it cost-effective to operate from a low-rent office outside of the capital beltway. More organizations may abandon assembling volunteer grass roots memberships and rely instead on mobilizing temporary mass audiences via paid ads, editorials, and radio and TV talk shows. Unlikely to change are the advocates' tools of access. As long as the officeholders worry about reelection, advocates will have to develop their personal and organizational credibility in ways that are sensitive to the constituent concerns of individual House members. Advocates will thus continue to capitalize on their commitment to the issues, their analyses of the issues and the players, and their capacities to supply politically useful contacts.

In the end, while some changes in House membership and rules have occurred since the time of this study, I am confident in speculating that there is sufficient stability in the political agenda, the institutional structures, and the incentives of officeholders to mitigate against any vast transformations in the patterns of leadership, access, and advocacy thus far described.

Implications for Future Research

By design and assumption, this research undertaking is distinct from others on congressional leadership and organized advocacy. I shall reflect on what we gain from these findings and what remains to be done. Imaginative readers will, I trust, arrive at additional observations and challenges that escape my attention.

Leadership

Most studies of congressional leadership begin with the individuals who hold formal positions of rank in the institution and observe how these particular individuals use their resources to build coalitions and pass (or halt) policy. This design, which relies on a random sample of professional lobbyists to identify those in the House who championed six major bills through Congress, allows even unranked individuals to appear among the leadership elite as long as their behavior warrants it. That the positions one holds in the institution come up nonetheless as an important predictor of leadership recognition is not a disappointment. It affirms that scholars are not misguided in focusing on prominent power brokers in Congress. Using title as the only selection criterion, after all, does capture a sizable cohort of the major players. And most of the accomplishments in our understanding of congressional leadership to date rest on these very important observations. Still, through unconventional means this investigation detects some new members of the leadership team, professional staff and unranked officeholders, who warrant further scholarly attention. Several next steps are in order.

First, what this study confirms but does not address in its particulars is the change that occurs in the number and characteristics of leaders over the course of the lawmaking cycle. Thus, one fruitful line of inquiry would be to identify how the determinants of leadership vary from one phase of policymaking to the next—agenda setting, formulation, and legitimation.[3]

That congressional staff emerge within the leadership elite is an important new finding that has consequences for enriching our understanding of politics. Two important follow-up questions come to mind. One pertains to the effect staff resources have on the leadership recognition of officeholders. Members of Congress have different numbers of staff, and they hire them to fulfill different functions. How do these management decisions of officeholders contribute to the officeholder's emergence in the leadership fold? A second line of inquiry pertains to the emergence of staff as leaders. One could address this question by examining the patrons, positions, and attributes of leading and nonleading staff.

Advocacy and Access

Studies of interest-group behavior seldom use an institutional and policy-oriented focus at one and the same time. The design, while time-consuming to implement, has much to endorse it. Here, for example, we determine that certain conditions about the policy domain (subject-matter complexity) and the political environment (public salience) discourage the involvement of some groups (citizen) and not others (occupational for-profits). It will take more than six policies to confirm the stability of this finding, but the evidence suggests an important new explanation of the occupational orientation that pervades most of promotional politics.

The overall size of the pressure-group community (whether 10, 100, or 1,000 groups organize to petition Congress) that mobilizes on a given issue varied, here, somewhat from one policy skirmish to the next. The difference in the size and complexion of the interest-group field, furthermore, corresponded positively with how broadly the policy was expected to reach into the American polity. This finding, if it withstands subsequent tests over numerous and varied issues, will help put to rest some lingering claims about the exclusive makeup of policy subsystems. If the scope of the issue dictates the number and diversity of players, then one is hard-pressed to accuse any specific decision makers of limiting the involvement of interested parties.

The design of this study offers an uncommon glimpse into the relative participation rates in promotional politics of publicly and privately sponsored agents. Within the public sector, two governmental jurisdictions dominated—the federal executive and state professional and trade associations. From the executive branch, both political appointees and career civil servants participated. The data reaffirm one previously identified aspect of the nature of political advocacy: Most groups that intervene in a policy debate have an occupational motive to do so. Trade associations, labor unions, and corporations dominate the pressure-group community when their economic turf is the subject of governmental intervention. When government representatives spar over the content of a bill, rest assured that occupational autonomy and budgets are being renegotiated as well.

What is new here is the division of labor, so to speak, between national and state-sponsored organizations. In trade policy, for example, where the president's autonomy was on the line, the president's lobbyists were the most visible governmental participants. Just the opposite occurred in the debate over welfare reform. Here, the state participants vastly outnumbered the administration's representatives on the Hill. More observation is needed to be confident about this pattern of involvement, but it appears from this preliminary view that governmental advocacy varies with the rights and resources that are under consideration.

Next, it comes as no surprise that bureaucrats and presidential appointees adopt different working styles toward members of Congress.

In keeping with the prevailing view, these data corroborate that civil servants eschew politics. In contrast, most presidential appointees behave strategically and pursue congressional leaders to advance their principal's interests. They behave like lobbyists from outside of government in their attention to interdepartmental coordination (coalition work in the private sector) and their practice of reaching out to leaders from both political parties. So little is known about the behind-the-scenes negotiations that transpire between Congress and the executive branch of government that almost any course of action would advance us intellectually. Scholars could, for example, follow up on the lobbyist's insight that divided government fosters bipartisan leadership arrangements in Congress. With the current trend toward one-term presidents, the condition of divided government is likely to recur and play into the hands of this research agenda.

Finally, with the exception of the previous section in which lobbyists reflected on their promotional work, generally, this has been a study of House leadership. The lessons learned here are nonetheless useful in speculating on senatorial leadership. In line with prominent works on the effects of bicameralism on legislative behavior (Baker 1989 and Fenno 1982), I expect both similarities and differences to surface. For example, it is reasonable to think that some senior Senate aides will attract the admiration and support of some rank-and-file senators. Also, with the diminished role of committees being what it is in this smaller, more informal chamber, it is highly plausible that some senators will join the ranks of the leadership elite with atypical committee portfolios. Senators, for example, often have the staff and the media outlets to become prominent spokespersons on an issue regardless of their committee base. Chamber rules, in particular the unanimous consent agreement and the filibuster, provide fewer procedural constraints than is the custom in the House. As a result, I expect party labels to make no difference in a senator's emergence as a leader, not even the initial and evanescent effect party was observed to command in the House.

Reassessment and Implications for Representative Government

Public confidence in Congress is at an all-time low. Opinion polls show that the low esteem for Congress is stable and widespread.[4] Editorials abound on the failure of the institution to behave responsibly. The savings and loan scandal and the more recent check-kiting fiasco are two debacles that received widespread attention in the media. These and similar events coincide with an unprecedented increase in calls for limiting the terms of congressional officeholders. According to many outspoken critics, the major problem is that Congress is "bought and paid for." Its members are thought to attend, first and foremost, to the interests of a well-heeled few who gain extraordinary access and influence through their social position, money, or organization. Others claim that record-high numbers of unelected staff deteriorate the representative function of Congress. As they see it, overburdened officials freely delegate important responsibilities to staff that they should retain for themselves. Such charges would be quite important if they were indeed true, but they are not well borne out by the evidence.

We return now to the three criticisms that first appeared in chapter 1 and evaluate each with the new insights supplied by this investigation.

First Claim: While the institution theoretically adheres to the majoritarian principle, real power rests in the hands of a small covey of elected leaders (party bosses and committee barons) who dictate solutions for others to follow.

Response: In keeping with conventional wisdom, on any one issue that wends its way through the institution, there are many more bystanders than there are players. The individuals looked to for steering policy, however, are not so few in number nor so homogeneous in perspective as critics may suppose. Alongside the names of prominent leaders (for example, the Speaker, majority leader, and minority leader) that would appear on everyone's list of heavy hitters are the names of some obscure officeholders and aides who hold no formal rank. Because the nature of the issues (their scope, complexity, and salience) dictates to some extent who will lead and who will follow, even those in the most alleged prominence may be temporarily stripped of their control. Consistent with everything we know about the institution, furthermore, both position and personal talent count for a lot in the making of a leader. However, when I investigate *which* positions and *what* personal attributes matter most, some new subtleties come to the fore. And the new evidence, while corroborating that influence is unevenly distributed, suggests promising courses of action for officeholders who want to hasten their ascent into the leadership fold.

Starting with the personal side of the ledger, one's tenure in the institution is decidedly correlated with leadership. Other individual characteristics such as political ideology and electoral vulnerability have no bearing on who becomes a leader in the first place. And, once individuals appear within the leadership elite, the majority party has no special claim on producing the leaders with the most recognition. The responsibility for championing important policies, if not equally borne, is borne nonetheless by Democrats and Republicans, political extremists and moderates, and officeholders with and without comfortable margins of electoral victory.

The data also substantiate that leadership recognition grows with legislators' capacities for knowing the subject matter and politics of the issues. What is more, the four personal attributes measured here are so inextricably connected with one another that their separate effects cannot be assessed. This is noteworthy because a naive observer, or politician for that matter, might guess that leaders gain prominence through specialization, demonstrating prowess in subject-matter negotiations or strategic gamesmanship but not both. The evidence from these data suggest that such is not the case. The individuals who inspire confidence in others because of their substantive expertise do not reportedly fall short in understanding and manipulating the politics of the situation.

In keeping with voluminous research on the subject, the evidence reaffirms two additional points: (1) The party hierarchies and the congressional committee spawn most of the named leaders, and in so doing the two structures sometimes vie for the attention of rank-and-file officeholders; and (2) The positions one holds in either or both of these structures correspond with varying levels of prominence. Individuals are particularly advantaged, for example, when they hold a formal party leadership post. Indeed, party leaders make up a large component of what I referred to in chapter 2 as the generalists, because they appear as key players over a wide array of disparate issues. Committee assignments are also important, and there is a new subtlety to consider. We saw in chapter 2 that many high-profile leaders who specialize in one or two policy areas often hold a seat on one of the five so-called prestige committees. In fact, lawmakers hold several seat assignments, and when bills are referred in such a way as to overlap with two or three of the legislators' vantage points, regardless of the committees' prominence, the legislators have a higher propensity to be recognized as leaders. In truth, committee appeal and jurisdictional breadth go hand in hand to some extent. So more than good fortune is involved in the incidence with which an officeholder's purview coincides with bill referral. Nonetheless, while I am not prepared to discount the importance of holding a seat on one of the big five committees, I conclude from these data that more needs to be made of the value certain combinations of seat assignments hold for their bearers.

In practice, this means that a legislator who sits on Agriculture, Judiciary, and Foreign Affairs—all committees having middling prestige—may have the maneuvering capabilities to champion more diverse issues than a member who sits on one highly regarded committee, such as

Appropriations or Ways and Means. To the extent that this is true, outspoken critics of the exclusivity of congressional power must revise their image of the politics of policy-making.

Beyond affording legislators the legitimacy to intervene and champion the causes they care about, it is through their committee assignments that members master the subject matter and politics of the situation. Elizabeth Wehr (1976) was correct to repeat the rank ordering a Republican leader assigned the committee chair, ranking minority member, and noncommittee members: "Jamie [L. Whitten] knows all. Sil[vio O. Conte] knows some. The average member knows zip." Committee assignments are the source of one additional resource that merits special attention— knowledgeable, enterprising staff, some share of whom belong themselves among the leadership elite. This discussion follows subsequently.

The final condition that affects individuals' chances for leadership pertains to features of the political environment and policy domain. In particular, the opportunities for being identified as a prominent leader increase somewhat when the subject matter of a bill is technically complex and arouses the interest of the mass public. When other factors are controlled for, the scope of the policy has little bearing on the recognition that accrues to leaders. The condition does, however, affect the diversity of champions the advocates choose to include in their Capitol Hill networks. For example, when issues are salient to the mass public, the advocates identify as leaders more Democrats, more party officers, and more officeholders than they do otherwise. Features of the issues and their decision-making environments, phenomena not easily controlled by anyone, affect the array of officials who are most in charge (chap. 4). Sometimes the effect is to broaden the cast of leaders, and sometimes it narrows it.

These data reaffirm several aspects about leadership in the U.S. House of Representatives. They also introduce some new complexities that erode simplistic notions about a rigid and predictable breakdown between the power-haves and power-have-nots.

Second Claim: Representatives abrogate the responsibilities for lawmaking that citizens entrust with them by deferring too often to experts among their staff and special-interest organizations.

Response: The facts are indisputable. Legislators are assisted by a vast array of individuals when they promulgate major policy. Unelected staff figure among the named leaders, confirming their prominence in the process. And while we do not have the House leaders' assessments of what the advocates contribute to the operation, the data reveal a highly permeable institution in which officeholders welcome and initiate contacts with hundreds of advocates who work on behalf of widely diverse organizational interests. In all of this give-and-take, do legislators abdicate authority? I think not.

The burden of shepherding controversial policy to passage is a collective undertaking in which officeholders look to their aides for substantial advice and assistance. On this there is no disagreement. According to the advocates, certain staff members are so competent at their jobs that they attract adherents from among the rank-and-file House membership. Furthermore, these special staff leaders comprise a healthy share (36 percent) of the entire cadre of named House leaders. This level of staff presence is stable across policies that vary considerably in subject-matter complexity and public salience. Nonetheless, there are important distinctions about staff leadership that restrain them relative to officeholders. First is the fact that 96 percent of staff leaders are identified along with their elected bosses. While staff play prominent roles, they do so only when their bosses are seriously committed to the initiative. Staff do not strike out on their own, championing policies that are of no interest to the officeholders who hire them. This coincidence of recognition is best interpreted as an extension, not an erosion, of the power of office.

Second, staff recognition is shallower and more narrowly focused than that of officeholders. Staff work from one base of operations (a congressional committee, a member's personal office, or a party leadership office), and their visibility to others is therefore limited relative to the officeholders who operate from several vantage points at once. Not surprisingly, of the six issues in this investigation, staff rarely gained prominence over more than two, and forte in only one area is more typical. Save one staff member who worked out of the Speaker's office, the individuals who preside over three or more disparate policies are all elected officials. In this way, the reach of staff leadership is constrained.

When it comes to the personal attributes that attend leadership, there are similarities and differences to report between officeholders and aides. For both groups, accessibility and substantive expertise are seen as being more important than political expertise and affability. While the differences are not pronounced, the officeholders scored higher than the aides on every dimension save accessibility. This result bolsters the impression that leading officeholders are in control of even the most complicated policy-making processes. If the data revealed that staff excelled over officeholders along the substantive and political dimensions or that more staff names appeared among the ranks of leaders when the issues became complex, I might conclude otherwise. That is, delegation is a weakness and a show of abdication of authority. Absent this information, it appears to me that leading officeholders share the responsibilities of policy-making because the task is too big to do alone. And when legislators defer to staff experts, they do so with the assurance that their trusted surrogates will carry out their wishes as if they had been there to do it themselves.[5]

Replace *oversight* with *policy-making* and Morris Ogul's (1976, 5) insight is as true today about congressional politics as it was when he first applied it to congressional-executive relations: "No amount of congressional dedication and energy, no conceivable increase in the size of committee staffs, and no extraordinary boost in committee budgets will enable the Congress to carry out its oversight obligations in a comprehensive and systematic manner. The job is too large for any combination of members and staff to master completely."

Out of necessity, members of Congress and their staffs rely on the energies, resources, and talents of numerous interested onlookers who are in the business of promoting their organization's interests. The condition gives rise to the next claim.

Third Claim: Unequal access translates into unequal influence, and members of Congress open their doors the widest to the monied crowd from corporate America.

Response: Of the three claims, this one is the easiest to dispute. The study includes a wide cross section of advocates from a plethora of organizations. While the groups differ substantially in the resources (e.g., money, members, credibility, affiliated PACs, experience, and expertise) they bring to their Capitol Hill partnerships, there is no evidence that supports the claim that House leaders are more accessible to some groups than others.

From the advocates' perspective, they adapt to their organizational strengths and weaknesses when approaching members of Congress. Those with large and diffused membership bases explain their ease in gaining access on the basis of their well-placed, politically relevant constituents and their organization's credibility. Advocates from memberless for-profit corporations emphasize their own credibility, not that of the organization, and the corporation's PAC. Advocates from citizen groups also mention their association's campaign involvement (PACs) but emphasize their knowledge of the issues. In this arrangement, no one is disadvantaged. The representatives of different organizations (occupational for-profit and nonprofit, grass roots citizen, and government) use different means, but their ends are remarkably similar. Regardless of their organizational affiliations and resources, in promotional politics, the advocates identify and assemble similar combinations of leaders.[6] The resources that open doors for them are reportedly as eclectic as the advocate's creativity allows.

The financial and nonfinancial aspects of political give-and-take are on a more even footing than critics would suspect. House leaders may need campaign money to get reelected, but to be granted a prominent role in shepherding policy, they need the political support of credible American institutions (church groups, labor unions, and trade associations), sophisticated analyses of pending initiatives that anticipate constituent concerns, allies who serve as confidants to undecided lawmakers, and novel perspectives that soften resistance and win approval. That House leaders reportedly received these valuable services from a wide cross section of interest groups tells me that the most conspicuous glad-handing lobbyists, whom commentators like to lionize and reproach, have no special claim to access nor to the provision of these services.

As an additional check on the alleged bias in the treatment that Congress gives different types of organizations, chapter 4 examined the gap between the advocates' ideal policy and what Congress enacted into law. With almost everyone reporting a 70 to 100 percent fit, the data corroborate numerous portrayals of an institution that is highly responsive to outside pressures. Furthermore, the advocates who are the least satisfied come from the organizations that allegedly have the closest contacts—the administration (through the revolving door) and the for-profit corporations (through money).[7] The dissatisfaction from the administration is not surprising when one considers that the lobbyists for Republican President Ronald Reagan were often at odds with the Democratic majority that controlled the Congress at the time. Perhaps both types of players pursued outcomes distant from the debated initiatives, so even sizable movement toward the advocates' preferred position on the policy continuum would not go far enough to close the gap and satisfy their expectations. Such a disparity in perspectives, if it were confined to the federal agencies and the for-profits, would account for the groups' dissatisfaction with the outcomes relative to other, more satisfied participants. Nonetheless, the low scores from the for-profit sector, in particular, counter the charge that members of Congress give these advocates special treatment. The fact that meagerly funded grass roots citizen groups come away as pleased, and oftentimes more pleased than other promotional groups, tells me that money is not the deciding factor in who gets what from Congress.

Last, the evidence corroborates something that has troubled interest-group scholars for decades—there is a bias to the interest-group community. Whereas occupational groups, in particular the nonprofits such as trade and professional associations, participate in great numbers almost without regard to the issues, citizen groups emerge in large numbers only sparingly (chap. 3). They arc most pronounced, for example, when the issues under consideration are sufficiently uncomplicated, first, to catch the attention of the media and, subsequently, to arouse public concern. Because so many problems that arrive on the congressional agenda are anything but simple, however, the leaders of citizens groups face organizational challenges that occupational groups do not.

While this inequity exists, it is not a problem that can easily be blamed on members of Congress. Indeed, the officeholders and aides, working from within the institution, provide the advocates, working within all sectors of the pressure community, valuable political intelligence (tips on the timing of key votes) and platforms (public hearings) with which to build personal and organizational credibility, two resources that are vital to institution building because they draw financial patronage and citizen volunteers. All of the advocates with whom I spoke described their partnerships with officeholders and staff as remarkably open and mutually beneficial. There is no evidence to support the claim, therefore, that politically valuable information is selectively parlayed to the groups with the biggest budgets or the most name-recognized board members.

Appendixes

Sample Selection

This study combines two methodologies that are often used in exclusion of one another. The first, the case study approach, allows close scrutiny of a limited number of events. Here, I narrow the focus to six specific policy-making endeavors, each with knowable political circumstances, to anchor the investigation into particular dynamics about leadership, access, and advocacy in the U.S. House of Representatives. Add to the case studies the survey method of interviewing a random selection of individuals who can verify what occurred during each conflict, and it is possible to test several propositions and to arrive at more general explanations of political behavior than could be achieved otherwise. The procedures for selecting the issues and the study participants are discussed in turn.

The Issues

To ensure that some amount of leadership and followership occurred, I biased the sample to include high-stakes issues where there is organized conflict, where the administration takes a public stand, and where there is closure.[1] *Congressional Quarterly Weekly*'s designation of "key" legislation identified a dozen or so issues that met most of these criteria. The six bills selected for inclusion in this study meet two additional criteria: (1) They reflect the assortment of subject matter typical of the national agenda, and (2) They were referred in such a way that all but three House committees became actively involved in their passage.

The selected policies, for example, possess international and domestic consequences. Foreign media outlets were particularly attentive to debates over limiting nuclear tests, funding the Nicaraguan Contras, and revamping international trade regulations. Farm credit reform and antidrug initiatives straddled domestic and international arenas, leaving welfare reform as the only bill with a distinctly domestic focus. Conflict, while common to them all, varied in focus and aroused varying levels of public interest. Some battles were primarily ideological, turning on core values about what properly remains in the public and private domains. Welfare reform is the best example of this. In contrast, the arguments over nuclear testing limits turned on technical feasibility more than ideology, and disputes over international trade and farm credit entailed both highly technical economic analyses and opinion over what is good or bad about government intervention. These and other diversities about the policies' subject matter and the controversies they aroused permit analysis into the identification of leaders and advocates under different and controlled circumstances.

Next, the omission of the committees on the District of Columbia, House Administration, and Interior and Insular Affairs is unlikely to jeopardize the identification of the true leaders of nationally focused lawmaking, because career politicians in Congress sit on six or more legislative panels (typically two full committees and four subcommittees). If a committee assignment, such as House Administration, is a poor platform from which to gain the expertise and visibility needed to lead important issues of the day, an officeholder's other committee positions will compensate for the inadequacy.

The Advocates

The sampling scheme for choosing advocates entailed a three-step process. From the public record, I drew up a preliminary list of all those who testified before the House committees and subcommittees that met to review the six policies. Next, I enlisted the assistance of several dozen congressional staff members who worked on the bills, either as committee and subcommittee professionals or as legislative assistants operating out of a member's office.[2]

Having observed the flow of advocates trafficking in and out of congressional offices and committee rooms during this period, the staffers were well equipped to refine the population frame. For example, it is a common practice for interest groups to send public luminaries and sympathetic citizens to testify before Congress, withholding their professional lobbyists for the behind-the-scenes work. Because it was these lobbyists and not the witnesses who oftentimes were capable of discriminating between leaders and followers in the House, the staff consultants were extremely valuable in, first, recognizing when such switches occurred and, then, providing the name of the appropriate advocate. Also, the staff members screened the witness lists to delete from the population frame any experts who they could confirm abstained from promotional politics. This removed the dispassionate experts who are ill equipped to comment on congressional leadership because they do not typically play proactive roles seeking out the movers of a bill.

Last, after grouping this refined list of names by issue and by sector (e.g., public, private for-profit, and private nonprofit), I drew a systematic random sample of 179 individuals, approximately 30 advocates per issue. Thirty individuals were eliminated from the final tally on the basis that they could not recall having played a meaningful promotional role (11 percent) or they refused to participate (6 percent) in the study. An additional 50 individuals (28 percent) could not be located for an interview. The remaining 97 advocates, 54 percent of the sampled participants, make up the final complement of respondents. These individuals represent the full spectrum of organizations that participated in crafting these laws, and, as I will argue, they closely resemble the distribution of groups that typically comprise the pressure-group community writ large.

The distributions in table A.1 allow us to examine the extent to which the current population and sample resemble that of a larger and possibly more universal interest-group community. Jack Walker's 1985 survey (1991) is particularly appealing for comparative purposes because its participants are not tied to particular events as are the participants in the current project. Rather, identification for his inquiry necessitated only that a group be mentioned in the 1984 edition of *Congressional Quarterly*'s *Washington Information Directory*. The differences in the Walker's and my designs are substantial and will no doubt result in some discrepancies, but I proceed cautiously with the comparison nonetheless.

The most remarkable similarity across the two interest-group communities is the extent to which the occupational groups dominate the scene. Using the sample figures from the current study, all but 26.9 percent

TABLE A.1. Cross-Study Comparison of Organizations by Sector and Type (in percentages)

	DeGregorio (1988)[a]		Walker (1984)
	$N = 97$	$N = 69$[b]	$N = 863$
For-profit	15.5	21.4	37.8
Nonprofit	18.6	25.7	32.5[c]
Citizen	28.9	26.9	23.9
State and Local	9.3	12.9	n.a.
Administration	26.8	n.a.	n.a.
Foreign	1.0	n.a.	n.a.
Mixed	n.a.	n.a.	5.8[d]

[a]The dates relate to the period in which the groups were documented to exist, not the intervals in which the interviews were conducted.

[b]The percentages in this column omit the 26 participants from the federal administration.

[c]This tally includes trade and professional associations from state and local government.

[d]The groups in this category have members from both the profit and nonprofit realms (J. Walker 1991, 60).

(the citizen category) of the groups have an occupational focus. In Walker's distribution, the occupational organizations constituted all but 23.9 percent of the distribution. The two studies also report comparable levels of participation from the nonprofit segment. Once we omit the federal officials from consideration and consolidate the state and local government associations with the private-sector nonprofits, as does Walker, we arrive at a proportion (38.6 percent) that is in line with his 33 percent figure (Walker 1991, 59).

In one regard the two pressure communities are different. Where the for-profit groups comprised nearly 38 percent of Walker's participants, they constitute only 21.4 percent of those in the current study. Two explanations of the discrepancy come to mind. First, both reports may be accurate in their portrayals of the advocacy community, and fewer for-profits are currently involved in promotional politics than in the mid-1980s. Second, and probably a more likely scenario, the bases on which individuals were selected to participate—the population frames of the two inquiries—create the difference. My method of interviewing congressional staff to identify the full complement of advocates who emerged to lobby the bills may have uncovered more obscure nonprofit and citizen-based organizations than obscure for-profit organizations, possibly biasing the overall distribution away from the for-profit community. The opposite skew (e.g., in favor of for-profit organizations) may have occurred as a result of Walker's near complete reliance on the *Washington Information Directory* (1984). If this interpretation is correct, the actual involvement of for-profit organizations in the advocacy community is somewhere between the two recorded figures, say 28 percent.

To account for the paucity of identified foreign lobbyists, I offer one possibility. Perhaps not many foreign officials take their causes directly to congressional leaders. This is the explanation offered by the one foreign national who participated in the study. In reflecting on the manner in which foreign officials approach Congress, he observed that most individuals use executive branch spokespersons as go-betweens. They filter their ideas and problems through allies in the administration, expecting them to have more clout in pressing their causes on the Hill. The respondent speculated that many individuals shy away from direct contact with congressional officials because the legislature is a difficult institution to comprehend and because in their own democracies they go to executive officials first and foremost.

APPENDIX 2

Leadership/Advocacy Study Instrument

DATE__/_/___
_ _ _ _ _   1. WHAT WAS YOUR INVOLVEMENT IN (BILL NUMBER) OF THE 100TH CONGRESS?
1 2 3 4 5   (Make note of quotable statements on a separate sheet of paper and
             circle the appropriate answers in the following clusters.)
code #

-            The respondent is:
6   1. lobbyist   4. presidential appointee
respoc   2. advocate   5. technical expert
             3. civil servant   6. other

-            The organization is:
7   1. profit   3. governmental
org. type   2. non-profit   4. quasi gov.
             5. other

_   2. WHAT WERE YOU TRYING TO ACHIEVE?
8   (Circle one of the following and record notable statements elsewhere.)
purpose
             1. weaken the bill as proposed
             2. support the bill as proposed
             3. strengthen the bill as proposed
             4. weaken some parts and strengthen other parts

. . .   3. CAN YOU SCORE YOURSELF, IN TERMS OF YOUR ACHIEVEMENTS, ON A ZERO TO 100 RATING SCALE?
9 10 11   IF YOU LOST GROUND THE SCORE WOULD BE A MINUS 1 TO 100.
             (Write a qualitative explanation of the score on a separate sheet of paper.)

             4. OPPORTUNITIES ARE QUITE LIMITED FOR UNELECTED INDIVIDUALS TO PARTICIPATE IN THE FORMAL
             LEGISLATIVE PROCESS. IN THESE INSTANCES WHEN DISCUSSIONS AND NEGOTIATIONS WERE CONFINED
             TO THE RESPONSIBLE ELECTED OFFICIALS ON THIS ISSUE, WHICH MEMBERS OF CONGRESS DID YOU GO
             TO FOR SUPPORT IN PURSUING YOUR CAUSE?I AM NOT CONCERNED WITH WHO YOU LOBBIED FOR A VOTE.
             I AM INTERESTED ONLY IN KNOWING THE NAMES OF THE SPECIAL FEW LEADERS WHOSE HELP YOU SOUGHT
             BECAUSE THEY HAVE AN INSIDE FOLLOWING (E.G., OTHER HOUSE MEMBERS LOOK TO THEM FOR GIVING
             VOTING CUES AND BUILDING COALITIONS.PROBE: AFTER THE RESPONDENT HAS FINISHED SPONTANEOUSLY
             LISTING INDIVIDUALS, ASK IF THEY CONSIDERED INDIVIDUALS FROM BOTH PARTIES, ALL COMMITTEES
             AND SUBCOMMITTEES, THE RULES COMMITTEE, THE FORMAL PARTY LEADERSHIP, AND INFORMAL CAUCUSES.

CHAMPIONS
_ _ _ 1_____   _ _ _ 11_____
_ _ _ 2_____   _ _ _ 12_____
_ _ _ 3_____   _ _ _ 13_____
_ _ _ 4_____   _ _ _ 14_____
_ _ _ 5_____   _ _ _ 15_____
_ _ _ 6_____   _ _ _ 16_____
_ _ _ 7_____   _ _ _ 17_____
_ _ _ 8_____   _ _ _ 18_____
_ _ _ 9_____   _ _ _ 19_____
_ _ _ 10_____   _ _ _ n _____

5. WHAT ATTRIBUTES DOES THIS (DO THESE) INDIVIDUAL (S) HAVE THAT YOU FIND ATTRACTIVE IN SHEPHERDING YOUR PERSPECTIVE ON THE ISSUE? (HAND THE RESPONDENT CARD ONE AND CIRCLE THE APPROPRIATE INDIVIDUALS NEXT TO EACH ATTRIBUTE.)

1 POSITION (CHAIR OF A RESPONSIBLE COMMITTEE)
2 POSITION (PARTY LEADERSHIP ROLE)
3 ACCESSIBILITY
4 AFFABILITY (EASE IN INTERPERSONAL RELATIONS)
5 SUBSTANTIVE EXPERTISE (KNOWS THE ISSUE BETTER THAN MOST)
6 POLITICAL EXPERTISE (KNOWS HOW TO BUILD A COALITION)
7 CONTACTS WITH A VALUABLE TARGET GROUP
8 "ONE OF US"
9 PASSIONATELY SUPPORTS THIS ISSUE
10 COMMANDS A FOLLOWING (WHEN S/HE SPEAKS, PEOPLE LISTEN)

ATTRIBUTES 1-10 INDIVIDUALS NAMED 1-n

		1 2 3 4 5 6 7 8 9 10 11 12 13 14 15 16 ...n
COMMITTEE POSITION	1.	1 2 3 4 5 6 7 8 9 10 11 12 13 14 15 16 ...n
LEADERSHIP POSITION	2.	1 2 3 4 5 6 7 8 9 10 11 12 13 14 15 16 ...n
ACCESS	3.	1 2 3 4 5 6 7 8 9 10 11 12 13 14 15 16 ...n
AFFABILITY	4.	1 2 3 4 5 6 7 8 9 10 11 12 13 14 15 16 ...n
SUBSTANTIVE EXPERTISE	5.	1 2 3 4 5 6 7 8 9 10 11 12 13 14 15 16 ...n
POLITICAL EXPERTISE	6.	1 2 3 4 5 6 7 8 9 10 11 12 13 14 15 16 ...n
CONTACTS	7.	1 2 3 4 5 6 7 8 9 10 11 12 13 14 15 16 ...n
US	8.	1 2 3 4 5 6 7 8 9 10 11 12 13 14 15 16 ...n
PASSION	9.	1 2 3 4 5 6 7 8 9 10 11 12 13 14 15 16 ...n
LISTENS	10.	1 2 3 4 5 6 7 8 9 10 11 12 13 14 15 16 ...n

PROBE: ARE THERE ANY OTHER CHARACTERISTICS THAT QUALIFIES THIS PERSON, IN YOUR EYES, TO SHEPHERD A BILL YOU CARE SO MUCH ABOUT?

6. HOW DID YOU GO ABOUT SECURING THE NEEDED ACCESS TO THIS PERSON(S)? (HAND THE RESPONDENT CARD 2.) CIRCLE NUMBERS BELOW SIGNIFYING CONGRESSMEN FROM ABOVE NEXT TO EACH AVENUE BELOW)

a PREVIOUS RELATIONSHIP (E. G. FORMER CONGRESSMAN OR HILL STAFFER) 1,2,3,..n
b PREVIOUS RELATIONSHIP (E.G. ADVOCATE OF A PRIOR ISSUE) 1, 2, 3,...n
c NETWORK VIA FRIEND/COLLEAGUE 1, 2, 3, 4, 5, 6, 7, 8, 9, 10, 11, ..n
d ESTABLISHED INDEBTEDNESS THROUGH SERVICE (E.G. INFORMATION, SPEECH-WRITING, ETC.) 1, 2, 3 ...n

e ESTABLISHED INDEBTEDNESS THROUGH CAMPAIGN WORK 1, 2, 3...n
f CONGRESSMAN SOUGHT OUT RESPONDENT 1, 2, 3...n
g OTHER 1, 2, 3, 4, 5, 6, 7, 8, 9, 10, 11...n

7. ARE THERE ANY CONGRESSMEN WHO YOU WOULD PREFER TO CHAMPION YOUR CAUSE, BUT
WHOM YOU DO NOT HAVE ACCESS TO? (IF NONE GO TO 9.) ____NO

8. WHAT IS IT ABOUT THESE PEOPLE THAT MAKES THEM SO DESIRABLE?

	ATTRIBUTES 1-10	INDIVIDUALS NAMED 1-6
	1 2 3 4 5 6...n	
COMMITTEE POSITION	1. 1 2 3 4 5 6...n	
LEADERSHIP POSITION	2. 1 2 3 4 5 6...n	
AFFABILITY	3. 1 2 3 4 5 6...n	
SUBSTANTIVE EXPERTISE	4. 1 2 3 4 5 6...n	
POLITICAL EXPERTISE	5. 1 2 3 4 5 6...n	
CONTACTS	6. 1 2 3 4 5 6...n	
PASSION	7. 1 2 3 4 5 6...n	
LISTENS	8. 1 2 3 4 5 6...n	

9. WHEN YOU THINK ABOUT YOUR EXPERIENCE OVER MANY ISSUES, NOT JUST THIS ONE, ARE
THERE ANY GENERAL RULES OF THUMB THAT YOU USE TO SELECT MEMBERS OF CONGRESS FOR
SHEPHERDING THE LEGISLATION YOU CARE ABOUT? (Circle all appropriate answers and
add new ones.)

1. positioned on the relevant committee
2. leadership position
3. keen interest
4. reliable (won't sell you down the river)
5. substantive expertise
6. political savvy
7. district link to the issue
8. other _____
9. other_____

10. DO INDIVIDUALS WHOSE HELP YOU SEEK VARY OVER THE LIFE-SPAN OF A BILL ON
(NAME ISSUE):

11. WHAT OTHER INSIGHTS WOULD YOU OFFER TO SOMEONE WHO IS JUST STARTING OUT
IN THIS BUSINESS (IN TERMS OF FINDING LEADERS ON CAPITOL HILL)?

5. WHAT ATTRIBUTES DOES THIS (DO THESE) INDIVIDUAL (S) HAVE THAT YOU FIND ATTRACTIVE IN SHEPHERDING YOUR PERSPECTIVE ON THE ISSUE?

        1 POSITION (CHAIR OF A RESPONSIBLE COMMITTEE)
        2 POSITION (PARTY LEADERSHIP ROLE)
        3 ACCESSIBILITY
        4 AFFABILITY (EASE IN INTERPERSONAL RELATIONS)
        5 SUBSTANTIVE EXPERTISE (KNOWS THE ISSUE BETTER THAN MOST)
        6 POLITICAL EXPERTISE (KNOWS HOW TO BUILD A COALITION)
        7 CONTACTS WITH A VALUABLE TARGET GROUP
        8 "ONE OF US"
        9 PASSIONATELY SUPPORTS THIS ISSUE
        10 COMMANDS A FOLLOWING (WHEN S/HE SPEAKS, PEOPLE LISTEN)

6. WHAT ATTRIBUTES DO YOU/YOUR ORGANIZATION POSSESS THAT MAKES YOU ATTRACTIVE TO THE LEADERS?

        1 PREVIOUS RELATIONSHIP (E. G. FORMER CONGRESSMAN OR HILL STAFFER)
        2 PREVIOUS RELATIONSHIP (E.G. ADVOCATE OF A PRIOR ISSUE)
        3 NETWORK VIA FRIEND/COLLEAGUE
        4 ESTABLISHED INDEBTEDNESS THROUGH SERVICE (E.G. INFORMATION, SPEECH-WRITING, ETC.)
        5 ESTABLISHED INDEBTEDNESS THROUGH CAMPAIGN WORK
        6 CONGRESSMAN SOUGHT OUT RESPONDENT
        7 OTHER

Notes

Chapter 1

1. Many political scientists emphasize that the ballot box is the single, most powerful tool that constituents have to make their representatives responsive to them (Huntington 1991, Mann 1978, Mayhew 1974, Riker 1965).

2. The identification of the leaders and their personal attributes comes from hourlong interviews with the participating advocates. Data in the public record on the lawmakers' positions, tenure, and electoral margins come from secondary sources such as Ehrenhalt, Amrine, and Duncan 1987 and Brownson 1987.

3. On February 26, 1987, the Tower Commission, appointed by Ronald Reagan to investigate the Iran-Contra scandal, issued its report. The president, while portrayed as disengaged from decision making and out of touch with his senior aides, was not directly implicated in any wrongdoing. "The portrait was devastating and shook Washington. . . . (But) Republicans insisted that the report exonerated Reagan because it did not pin knowledge and responsibility on him" (Barry 1989, 139).

4. Policies differ in the technical complexity of their subject matter, the breadth of their reach into society, and the interest with which they are reported in the media and received by the public. These are some of the features of the issues themselves that affect who participates in the process, either as leaders or as advocates (Rohde 1991, Price 1978, Manley 1966).

5. "Ever since 1983, Contra aid has been one of the most divisive issues on Capitol Hill. But it has rarely been a strictly party-line issue. In both chambers a significant minority of Democrats have supported President Reagan's requests for aid to the Nicaraguan guerrillas, and smaller minorities of Republicans have opposed the President" (Rapp 1988). The House on February 3 rejected H. J. Res. 444, by a slim margin 211–219: R 164–12; D 47–207, Reagan's request for $36.25 million for military aid to the Contras. In late March, following the signing of a cease-fire agreement between the Nicaraguan government and the Contras, Congress cleared $47.9 million for nonmilitary aid to assist the victims of the Nicaraguan civil war and to sustain the rebels until the new U.S. administration under George Bush crafted its own policy toward the region.

6. Of the six bills, the one to limit nuclear testing was the only one to fail passage in the Senate and thus reach no audience at all. While under debate, however, this policy purported to affect a small or a large audience, depending on one's per-

spective. In the short term, it affected only a few scientists and a clique of politicians in the United States and the Soviet Union. In the long term, it had the potential to affect the use of nuclear weapons and thus the safety of people throughout the world.

7. This qualitative characterization of the scope of the respective bills, moreover, perfectly corresponds with the number of indexing terms that the Library of Congress uses to identify the initiatives in their on-line location service. Omnibus drug captures the high of 471 terms, and Contra aid captures the low of 11. Indeed, there is a gap in excess of 100 indexing terms separating the bills characterized here as narrow and broad.

8. Interview, July 19, 1991.

9. Interview, June 22, 1992.

10. The substantive difference occurs as well when we compare the total coverage four major newspapers gave each policy in the months surrounding passage. While omnibus trade and Contra aid are above the median (75 stories), Contra aid is a clear outlier with 543 stories.

11. With the national agenda as replete as it is with multipurpose, technically complex laws that affect widely disparate audiences, it is no wonder that the outreaches occur as a necessary aspect of lawmaking. Legislative leaders must be able to argue the issue from many different perspectives. They need to be fully apprised of what their supporters as well as their opponents are saying about the feasibility and ramification of pending initiatives. Not knowing the full picture leaves them blindsided and less capable of manipulating the opinions of the rank-and-file officeholders whose votes they are attempting to win. While congressional staff supply some of this information, they too rely on the advocates for technical know-how and political insights.

12. Twenty individuals eliminated themselves at this juncture on the basis that their involvement was minimal or lacking in promotional content.

13. In preparation for the scheduled interview, the respondents were sent two lists of attributes, one pertaining to congressional leaders and the other pertaining to their own credentials and those of their organizations. The practice facilitated the interview process and ensured that every respondent reflected on the merits of a comparable set of factors. While many factors did not suit particular leaders (or advocates), the participants rarely found it necessary to add attributes not included in the lists.

14. Since November 1994, the number of Republicans has swelled slightly as a few disaffected Democrats switched party affiliation.

Chapter 2

1. This particular excerpt was taken from a lecture to students at the American University. Dr. Walker lectures widely to such groups as the American League for Lobbyists, and he teaches a course entitled "Economic and National Security Pol-

icy Making: How Government Really Works" at the University of Texas at Austin. His power and access on Capitol Hill are renowned (Berry 1989, Nader and Taylor 1986, Drew 1991).

2. Candidates for Congress compete for one seat per district, single-member races as opposed to at-large races. The only incumbents to race against each other, therefore, are the unfortunate few who, due to a shift in population, must compete for one seat where there were once two. Redistricting decisions happen only once every ten years following the national census.

3. The power of majority status is driven home by Holly Idelson (1995).

4. Stewart McKinny (R-Connecticut) died in 1987. As a consequence, much of the subsequent analysis uses a base of 434 instead of 435. The difference in N does not affect this calculation of Democratic seats held.

5. These transfer data are very instructive in revealing trends in committee appeal over time, as well as in making static comparisons. Here we are particularly interested in the stability of committee appeal, so we use the net transfer dominance rankings reported in Bullock and Sprague 1972. These data span a 10-year period, concluding with the 99th Congress. More recent cross-sectional analysis, available in Smith and Deering 1990, departs little from these long-trend figures.

6. A partial list includes: Speaker James Wright (D-Texas), Democratic Caucus Chair Richard Gephardt (D-Missouri), Minority Leader Robert Michel (R-Illinois), Majority Whip Tony Coelho (D-California), Majority Leader Thomas Foley (D-Washington), Republican Conference Chair Richard Cheney (R-Wyoming), Republican Chief Deputy Whip Edward Madigan (R-Illinois), and Minority Whip Trent Lott (R-Mississippi).

7. The staff leaders are excluded from this analysis because explanatory data are not available on those who are not recognized as leaders. In contrast, the public record provides useful measures on all elected officials (e.g., tenure, electoral vulnerability, ideology).

8. The lobbyists assessed each of the named leaders along four dimensions: accessibility, affability, substantive expertise, and political expertise. When these dichotomous scores are added up for individual leaders (as many as 22 lobbyists name the same leader in independent interviews), we obtain a measure of the personal talents that the advocates associate with representative X's leadership style. In preparation for factor analysis, I standardized the measure of attributes across identified leaders by dividing the frequency of each attribute by the total number of times the leader was named by the study participants. The factor scores that are included in the regression analysis include only two of the four dimensions, however. I eliminated accessibility because almost every named leader is described as possessing this attribute, and this lack of variation could suppress the effect the other talents have on leadership. I eliminated affability because a sizable proportion of respondents declined to make this assessment. The factor analyses are included below. In each case, they confirm that the personal attributes are sufficiently correlated with one another to form a single analytical dimension for use in the regression equation.

Personal Attribute	Four Measures Entered Factor Score	Two Measures Entered Factor Score
Accessibility	.715	n.a.
Substantive Expertise	.688	.930
Political Expertise	.530	.843
Affability	.359	n.a.

Note: Entries are factor weights after varimax rotation, a solution that maximizes the variance of the loadings.

9. My focus is on individuals in Congress and the ways expertise affects leadership. For an excellent macrolevel analysis of congressional specialization, its origins and implications on legislative efficiency, see Krehbiel 1991.

Chapter 3

1. In the pages that follow I employ a classification system previously used by Jack Walker (1991) and Jeffrey M. Berry (1989). They split the private, nongovernmental sector into two main divisions: occupational and nonoccupational. Nonoccupational groups appeal to broad categories of people who share an interest that is unrelated to any one line of work. These are more popularly known as cause-oriented, citizen-based groups. The National Organization for Women, the American Association of Retired Persons, and the Urban League are examples. The occupational groups have members who usually share a common occupational interest. Trade and professional associations and labor unions belong to this category, including, by way of example, the Pharmaceutical Manufacturers Associations, United Mine Workers, and the AFL-CIO. Within the occupational category, furthermore, there are for-profits and nonprofits.

2. The Treasury aides, it was believed, could negotiate a tougher stance on behalf of the president because they could say no to the powerful agriculture lobbies (interview, June 12, 1992).

3. Interviews, June 11 and 12, 1992.

4. Interview, October 15, 1992.

5. Close, Bologna, and McCormick (1989, 3) put the number at 12,500, with the following substantive breakdown. "The largest element (about 3,700) are officers of the 1,900 trade and professional associations and labor unions which keep permanent offices in the Nation's Capital. Another 1,500 are representatives of individual corporations who, as distinguished from their marketing colleagues, are responsible for government and public relations. About 2,500 are advocates of special causes from ERA to environment, from handgun control to prison reform, from saving whales to saving unborn children. Lawyers and consultants who have registered as lobbyists or foreign agents or who have been identified as representing clients in regulatory matters and legal confrontations with government currently number 3,200."

6. Jack Walker (1991) finds this same trend and uses as an example the tobacco industry, which organized a powerful lobby to protect itself from unwanted government intervention.

7. For a provocative counterargument, see Mueller 1992.

8. James Pfiffner (1994) assembles recent data on executive branch personnel: White House (400–500), Executive Office of the President (1,700), the cabinet (14), and the federal bureaucracy (3 million—sans military).

9. The cycle is characterized as having two phases. First, the relative newcomers are suspicious and hostile toward the legions of professionals they are supposed to oversee. After working closely together for two or three years, their suspicions give way to mutual respect and trust.

10. The modern Office of Congressional Relations was fashioned to a large extent by Larry O'Brien under Presidents Kennedy and Johnson (Patterson 1980).

11. These impressions come from many personal encounters with a variety of civil servants (GS 15 and above), who reported their experiences and goals for service to students enrolled in the Washington Semester Program of The American University (1988–1990).

12. The complete table was reported in Pfiffner 1988.

13. The comparison figures reported in appendix 1 are from his 1985 survey of 1,636 groups indexed in the *Washington Information Directory*. Of this number he received 863 responses. For a thorough description of his sampling methodology, see J. Walker 1991.

14. Most studies about pressure-group politics focus on privately sponsored (e.g., nongovernmental) endeavors that have a public policy mission, and they label them "public interest" organizations. In the pages that follow, I break from this pattern and distinguish between public and private enterprises based on their primary auspices. Government-sponsored entities are in the public domain, while privately sponsored associations, even nonprofit ones, are in the private domain. Although groups within the private sector, such as the Children's Defense Fund, the Center for International Policy, and Physicians for Social Responsibility, receive varying levels of encouragement, financial support (grants and contracts), and subsidies (breaks on mailing rates and taxes) from the government, their spokespersons represent private views and private interests. Public-sector advocates, by contrast, represent elected officials (the National Association of Governors, the National League of Cities), public employees (the American Federation of State, County, and Municipal Employees, the Brotherhood of Chiefs of Police), and the providers of government services (American Public Welfare Association). Each of these groups, in turn, would argue that they also represent the constituents (or service recipients) to whom they are accountable.

15. This illustration focuses on discordance among state and local participants, but I should note that federal agencies had unique and conflicting perspectives as well. For the U.S. Coast Guard to improve its capacity for interdiction, for example, its representatives argued for more money and an enlarged mandate, putting it at odds with other federal agencies.

16. Interviews, July 12 and July 31, 1991.

17. Interview, September 1, 1991.

18. There are exceptions to this rule, as is the case with the farmer cooperatives in this study.

19. The evidence on the degree to which differences in organization type correspond with resource acquisition (e.g., members, money, staff) and political access is presented in the next chapter.

20. Interviews, October 17 and November 1, 1991.

21. There are many ways of characterizing the conflict that emerged over the trade bill. Elizabeth Wehr (1988, 305) offers the perspective of Hank Brown (R-Colorado), who sympathized with the president's fear that the bill would threaten his autonomy. "The mandatory trade reductions are so awful, Brown said, that the executive branch and recalcitrant trading partners would be forced into useful trade negotiations to avoid them. 'We just use our markets as leverage.' . . . The legislation puts them on the spot. 'It forces them to go on record when they take one of the ways out. They don't like it and I don't blame 'em.' The real fight, in Brown's view, is not over trade policy but over presidential accountability."

22. Interviews, June 24 and July 15, 1991, and January 20, 1992.

23. Many complicated bills having to do with, for example, welfare, the environment, and international trade policy require several years of working and reworking before support mounts around one preferred solution. Two examples with which the reader is probably already familiar are the Clean Air Act of 1991 and the North American Free Trade Agreement (NAFTA). The deliberation on the first of these policies consumed well over a decade (Cohen 1992), and the trade debate, which dominated much of the 1992 presidential campaign between George Bush and Bill Clinton, got its start in the 1930s (Lewis 1993).

24. The data come from two sources: Ruffner 1988 and *Public Interest Profiles* 1988.

25. According to this spokesperson, the president supported the bailout and restructuring provisions of the legislation, but he wanted to keep the costs to a minimum (first interview, June 12, 1992). Since the bill had more to do with banking practices than agricultural policy, the Treasury Department looked like a good agency to champion the president's position. Furthermore, having no relations to engender within the farming community took leverage away from lobbyists who in years past were known to wrap the FCA around their little finger (second interview, June 12, 1992).

26. In the struggle to elevate Clarence Thomas to the Supreme Court, for example, I found a strong relationship between the groups' reliance on coalitions and the organizations' staff size and member base (DeGregorio and Rossotti 1995). That time, the advocates reported on their groups' "active" membership as a share of the total membership. Saying nothing about causality, the correspondence was clear. The groups with the largest share of active citizens were those with sizable staffs. Moreover, these were the organizations, more often than not, that participated in coalition work.

Chapter 4

Epigraph source: Berry 1989, 163.

1. In this study the respondents, all advocates, were asked to single out only officeholders and aides whom they selected as leaders because of the individuals' recognizable following inside the House. In John W. Kingdon's (1981) study, the respondents, all officeholders, reported on the factors they considered and the people (e.g., colleagues, constituents, staff) they consulted in preparation for an upcoming vote. Because of the dissimilarity in the studies' foci, leadership on the one hand and decision making on the other, the named individuals and their attributes will overlap only to the degree that Kingdon's respondents took cues from House leaders. This happened every time the decision makers deferred to colleagues and staff members who served as cue givers to a number of House members other than themselves. When cue givers have a very personal or restricted following that would go unnoticed by an attentive observer, chances are they do not meet my definition of a leader. The other disjunction between Kingdon's emphasis and my own is that cue givers can and do reside outside the institution's walls (e.g., administration officials, constituents, lobbyists). By definition and practice, House leaders all reside within the institution.

2. For an excellent review of the literature on this subject, see Rieselbach 1992.

3. A fourth goal comes into the picture only sporadically. When elected officials aspire to achieve a higher office (e.g., a move from House to Senate, a move from the Senate to the White House), they behave strategically with the interests of their new audience in mind (Fenno 1973).

4. Also, House rules give the party holding the majority of seats some procedural advantages that, when applied adroitly, are capable of coercing compliance, a technique not encountered in most advocacy groups save maybe labor unions.

5. For a lucid discussion of this reasoning, see Arnold 1990.

6. In *The Active Society,* Amitai Etzioni (1968) discussed two dimensions of three types of power—coercive, utilitarian and normative. The first dimension has to do with the speed with which the compliance occurs. The second pertains to the longevity of the compliance. Coercive approaches have the most immediate effects, and compliance is generally short lived. Just the opposite occurs with normative approaches such as education. When followers begin to value the same outcomes as those wielding power, the leaders have little to fear from future defection. Utilitarian methods of attracting a following reside somewhere along the middle of these continua. Compliance is likely to be quicker than with normative approaches of influence and less long lasting.

7. The Democrats' control of the agenda and the Republicans' 40-year status as a minority party undermined bipartisan give-and-take in the House. Janet Hook (1986) provides some background on the subject. Also, Cohen 1994 is a highly readable account of blocking procedures and their implications on the players, the politics, and the policies.

8. House insiders refer to the document as "the chairman's mark," making no secret of its authorship and its likely biases. The latter are tempered, however,

because as staff assemble the key provisions for committee approval, they are careful to include at least some provisions that their opponents want (DeGregorio 1987).

9. For a detailed analysis of how legal status constrains the range of groups' activities, see Shaiko 1991 and Berry 1984.

10. Schlozman and Tierney (1986) report two different figures—58 percent of their survey participants contributed financially to political campaigns with the intention of gaining influence, yet only 24 percent of the same groups provided endorsements and volunteers. By Jack Walker's (1991) account, only 22.4 percent of interest groups participate in promotional politics through "electioneering" (109). He does not distinguish between financial and nonfinancial involvement.

11. For some excellent articles on the organization, regulation, and consequences of political action committees, see Wright 1989, Gopoian 1984, Sorauf 1988, and Conway 1991.

12. In an internal document, Common Cause reports the existence of 34 House leadership PACs in 1987–88. A sample is included for illustrative purposes. The legislators' surnames are listed parenthetically: Pax Americas (Bonior), Congressional Black Caucus PAC (Clay), House Leadership Fund (Foley), Committee for the 100th Congress (Rangel), Independent Action (Udall), and Conservatives for Hope and Opportunity (Gingrich).

13. For an extensive discussion of this point, see R. Smith 1995.

14. Interviews, September 13, 1992, and June 21, 1991.

15. Interview, September 13, 1991.

16. Campaign work and professional service have three features in common: (1) They anticipate a future response based on current behavior; (2) Both employ a quid pro quo mentality—I help you and you help me; and (3) Neither bears directly on a known, pending policy initiative.

17. Interview, April 9, 1991.

18. In this sample farmer cooperatives are counted among the for-profit organizations. These member-based groups account for the for-profits' outstanding showing on this dimension. So it is an artifact of coding that citizen-based groups do not excel on this dimension.

Chapter 5

1. See appendix 1, questions 9–11, for the exact wording of the questions on which this discussion is based.

2. For an excellent analysis of the complexities that attend agenda setting, see Kingdon 1984.

3. See chapter 2 in Vogler 1993.

4. "In 19 surveys over the last five years, spanning three congresses and two presidents, the average scores for Congress have been 33 percent approval and 62 percent disapproval." This statement appeared in a *Washington Post* lead article entitled "Lawmakers Face Deep Cynicism," sec. A1, p. 3, 3 July 1994.

5. For a good discussion of the closeness of the staff-member policy-making

partnerships, see DeGregorio 1988. For a discussion of the delegation practices of lawmakers to aides, see DeGregorio 1994.

6. When multivariate analysis is used to estimate the effects that the advocates' personal talents (credibility, in-kind service, career experience), the organizational resources (membership size, credibility, budget), and the nature of the policy (salience, complexity, and scope) have on several measures of the advocates' access (e.g., the total number of leaders they named as well as the proportion of the named leaders who are Democrats, officeholders, and party leaders), the results are unenlightening. A negligible amount of the variation is explained, and organizational resources appear not to matter at all.

7. Evidence from this study contradicts the conventional wisdom that corporations are the wealthiest of advocates. Rather, they are positioned somewhere between the least-endowed citizen groups and the most-endowed occupational nonprofit groups. See chapter 4.

Appendix 1

1. During this two-year period the House passed 1,061 bills, 713 of which were public laws approved in both chambers (Ornstein, Mann, and Malbin 1990). The overwhelming majority of these bills were eliminated from consideration because they attracted no controversy. With no information in the public record to refute it, I can only surmise that these were relatively trivial matters that did not call for leaders skillful in the art of coalition building. Others may disagree, but I maintain that there is no leadership to observe when all lawmakers hold the same opinions about what to pass and what to foil, as they contemplate the legislative agenda.

2. I approached only professional staff members who held senior positions on the committees and subcommittees to which the bills were referred back in 1987 and 1988. These individuals suggested that I enlist the help of an additional handful of legislative assistants who they knew would be familiar with the advocacy that had taken place around these bills.

References

Arnold, R. Douglas. 1990. *The Logic of Congressional Action.* New Haven: Yale University Press.

Bach, Stanley, and Steven S. Smith. 1988. *Managing Uncertainty in the House of Representatives.* Washington, D.C.: Brookings Institution.

Backstrom, Charles H., and Gerald Hursh-Cesar. 1981. *Survey Research,* 2d ed. New York: Wiley.

Baker, Ross. 1989. *House and Senate.* New York: W. W. Norton.

Barnard, Chester I. 1968. *The Functions of the Executive.* Cambridge: Harvard University Press.

Barry, John. 1989. *The Ambition and the Power.* New York: Viking Press.

Bennis, Warren G. 1989. *On Being a Leader.* Reading, Mass.: Addison-Wesley.

Berry, Jeffrey M. 1989. *The Interest Group Society,* 2d ed. Glenview, Ill.: Scott, Foresman; Little, Brown.

———. 1984. *The Interest Group Society.* Boston: Little, Brown.

———. 1977. *Lobbying for the People.* Princeton: Princeton University Press.

Bianco, William T. 1994. *Trust: Representatives and Constituents.* Ann Arbor: University of Michigan Press.

Bisnow, Mark. 1990. *In The Shadow of the Dome.* New York: Morrow.

Bosso, Christopher J. 1991. "Adaption and Change in the Environment Movement." In *Interest Group Politics,* 3d ed. Edited by Allan J. Cigler and Burdett A. Loomis. Washington, D.C.: Congressional Quarterly Press.

Browne, William P. 1990. "Organized Interests and Their Issue Niches: A Search for Pluralism in a Policy Domain." *Journal of Politics* 52:477–509.

———. 1986. "Policy and Interests: Instability and Change in a Classic Issue Subsystem." In *Interest Group Politics,* 2d ed. Edited by Allan J. Cigler and Burdett A. Loomis. Washington, D.C.: Congressional Quarterly Press.

Brownson, Charles B. 1987. *Congressional Staff Directory.* Mt. Vernon, Va.: Staff Directories, Ltd.

Bullock, Charles S. III. 1972. "Freshmen Committee Assignments and Re-election in the U.S. House of Representatives." *American Political Science Review* 66:996–1007.

Bullock, Charles S. III, and David W. Brady. 1983. "Party, Constituency and Roll-Call Voting in the U.S. Senate." *Legislative Studies Quarterly* 8:29–43.

Bullock, Charles S. III, and John Sprague. 1972. "A Research Note on the Committee Reassignment of Southern Democratic Congressmen." *Journal of Politics* 34:493–512.

165

Canon, David T. 1989. "The Institutionalization of Leadership in the U.S. Congress." *Legislative Studies Quarterly* 14:415–44.

Cherryholmes, Cleo H., and Michael J. Shapiro. 1969. *Representatives and Roll Calls.* Indianapolis: Bobbs-Merrill.

Cigler, Allan J. 1986. "From Protest Group to Interest Group: The Making of American Agriculture Movement, Inc." In *Interest Group Politics,* 2d ed. Edited by Allan J. Cigler and Burdett A. Loomis. Washington, D.C.: Congressional Quarterly Press.

Cigler, Allan J., and Burdett A. Loomis, eds. 1995. *Interest Group Politics,* 4th ed. Washington, D.C.: Congressional Quarterly Press.

———. 1991. *Interest Group Politics,* 3d ed. Washington, D.C.: Congressional Quarterly Press.

———. 1986. *Interest Group Politics,* 2d ed. Washington, D.C.: Congressional Quarterly Press.

———. 1983. *Interest Group Politics.* Washington, D.C.: Congressional Quarterly Press.

Clausen, Aage R. 1973. *How Congressmen Decide: A Policy Focus.* New York: St. Martin's Press.

Close, Arthur C., Gregory L. Bologna, and Curtis W. McCormick. 1989. *Washington Representatives.* New York: Columbia Books.

Cloud, David S. 1995. "GOP, to Its Own Great Delight, Enacts House Rules Changes." *Congressional Quarterly Weekly Report* 53:13–14.

Cohen, Richard E. 1994. *Changing Course in Washington: Clinton and the New Congress.* New York: Macmillan College Publishing Co.

———. 1992. *Washington at Work: Back Rooms and Clean Air.* New York: Maxwell Macmillan International.

Congressional Quarterly. 1979. *Washington Information Directory 1980–81.* Washington, D.C.: Congressional Quarterly.

———. 1984. *Washington Information Directory 1984–85.* Washington, D.C.: Congressional Quarterly.

Congressional Research Service. 1986. *Congress and Pressure Groups: Lobbying in a Modern Democracy.* Washington, D.C.: Government Printing Office.

Conway, Margaret M. 1991. "PACS in the Political Process." In *Interest Group Politics,* 3d ed. Edited by Allan J. Cigler and Burdett A. Loomis. Washington D.C.: Congressional Quarterly Press.

Cooper, Joseph, and David W. Brady. 1981. "Institutional Context and Leadership Style: The House from Cannon to Rayburn." *American Political Science Review* 75:411–25.

Davidson, Roger H. 1992. *The Postreform Congress.* New York: St. Martin's Press.

———. 1988. "The New Centralization on Capital Hill." *Review of Politics* 49:345–64.

DeGregorio, Christine. 1995. "Patterns of Senior Staff Use in Congressional Committees." *Polity* 28:261–75.

———. 1994. "Professional Committee Staff as Policymaking Partners in the U.S. Congress." *Congress and the Presidency* 21:49–65.

———. 1993. "Leadership Approaches in Congressional Committee Hearings." *Western Political Quarterly* 45:971–83.

———. 1988. "Professionals in the U.S. Congress: An Analysis of Working Styles." *Legislative Studies Quarterly* 13: 459–76.

———. 1987. Professional staff members in Congress: A subcommittee perspective. Ph.D. diss., University of Rochester.

DeGregorio, Christine, and Jack Rossotti. 1995. "Campaigning for the Court: Interest Group Participation in the Bork and Thomas Confirmation Processes." In *Interest Group Politics,* 4th ed. Edited by Allan J. Cigler and Burdett A. Loomis. Washington, D.C.: Congressional Quarterly Press.

Dodd, Lawrence C., and Bruce I. Oppenheimer. 1993a. "Maintaining Order in the House: The Struggle for Institutional Equilibrium." In *Congress Reconsidered,* 5th ed. Edited by Lawrence C. Dodd and Bruce I. Oppenheimer. Washington, D.C.: Congressional Quarterly Press.

Dodd, Lawrence C., and Bruce I. Oppenheimer, eds. 1993b. *Congress Reconsidered,* 5th ed. Washington, D.C.: Congressional Quarterly Press.

Dodd, Lawrence C., and Bruce I. Oppenheimer. 1989a. "Consolidating Power in the House: The Rise of a New Oligarchy." In *Congress Reconsidered,* 4th ed. Edited by Lawrence C. Dodd and Bruce I. Oppenheimer. Washington, D.C.: Congressional Quarterly Press.

Dodd, Lawrence C., and Bruce I. Oppenheimer, eds. 1989b. *Congress Reconsidered,* 4th ed. Washington, D.C.: Congressional Quarterly Press.

Drew, Elizabeth. 1991. "Charlie." In *Interest Group Politics,* 3d ed. Edited by Allan J. Cigler and Burdett A. Loomis. Washington, D.C.: Congressional Quarterly Press.

Ehrenhalt, Alan, Renee Amrine, and Philip D. Duncan. 1987. *Politics in America: The 100th Congress.* Washington, D.C.: Congressional Quarterly Press.

Etzioni, Amitai. 1968. *The Active Society: A Theory of Societal and Political Processes.* New York: Free Press.

Evans, Charles L. 1991. *Leadership in Committee.* Ann Arbor: University of Michigan Press.

Evans, Diana M. 1991. "Lobbying the Committees: Interest Groups and the House Public Works and Transportation Committee." In *Interest Group Politics,* 3d ed. Edited by Allan J. Cigler and Burdett A. Loomis. Washington, D.C.: Congressional Quarterly Press.

Fenno, Richard. 1991. *Emergence of a Senate Leader: Pete Domenici and the Reagan Budget.* Washington, D.C.: Congressional Quarterly Press.

———. 1982. *The United States Senate: A Bicameral Perspective.* Washington, D.C.: American Enterprise Institute for Policy Research.

———. 1978. *Home Style: House Members in Their Districts.* Glenview, Ill.: Scott, Foresman.

———. 1973. *Congressman in Committees.* Boston: Little, Brown.

Fiorina, Morris P. 1977. *Congress, Keystone of the Washington Establishment.* New Haven: Yale University Press.

Fiorina, Morris P., and Kenneth A. Shepsle. 1989. "Formal Theories of Leadership: Agents, Agenda Setters, and Entrepreneurs." In *Leadership and Politics,* edited by Bryan D. Jones. Lawrence: University Press of Kansas.

Fowler, Linda, and Robert D. McClure. 1989. *Political Ambition: Who Decides to Run for Congress.* New Haven: Yale University Press.

Fox, Harrison W., and Susan Webb Hammond. 1977. *Congressional Staff: The Invisible Force in American Lawmaking.* New York: Free Press.

Gopoian, David J. 1984. "What Makes PACs Tick? An Analysis of Allocation Patterns of Economic Interest Groups." *American Journal of Political Science* 28:259–81.

Hager, George. 1993a. "Mercurial vs. Imperturbable: Kasich and Sabo Square Off." *Congressional Quarterly Weekly Report* 51:654–55.

———. 1993b. "House Democrats Easily Back Clinton Budget Blueprint." *Congressional Quarterly Weekly Report* 51:653.

Hall, Richard L. 1993. "Participation, Abdication, and Representation in Congressional Committees." In *Congress Reconsidered,* 5th ed. Edited by Lawrence C. Dodd and Bruce I. Oppenheimer. Washington, D.C.: Congressional Quarterly Press.

———. 1992. "Measuring Legislative Influence." *Legislative Studies Quarterly* 17:205–32.

Hall, Richard L., and Lawrence C. Evans. 1990. "The Power of Subcommittees." *Journal of Politics* 52:335–55.

Hall, Richard L., and Frank W. Wayman. 1990. "Buying Time: Moneyed Interests and the Mobilization of Bias in Congressional Committees." *American Political Science Review* 84:797–820.

Hammond, Susan W. 1990. "Committee and Informal Leaders in the U.S. House of Representatives." In *Leading Congress: New Styles and Strategies,* edited by John Kornacki. Washington, D.C.: Congressional Quarterly Press.

Hansen, John Mark. 1985. "The Political Economy of Group Membership." *American Political Science Review* 79:79–96.

Herrnson, Paul S. 1990. "Campaign Professionalism and Fundraising in Congressional Elections." *Western Political Quarterly* 42:301–23.

Herrnson, Paul S., Clyde Wilcox, and Robert Biersack, eds. 1994. *Risky Business? PAC Decisionmaking in Congressional Elections.* Armonk, N.Y.: M. E. Sharpe.

Hiatt, Fred, and Margaret Shapiro. 1988. "Dukakis-Bentsen Ticket Elicits Trade Anxiety in Tokyo." *Washington Post,* 16 July, A18.

Hirschman, Albert O. 1970. *Exit, Voice and Loyalty.* Boston: Harvard University Press.

Hojnacki, Marie. Forthcoming. "Interest Groups' Decisions to Join Alliances." *American Journal of Political Science.*

Hook, Janet. 1988. "Jim Wright: Taking Big Risks to Amass Power." *Congressional Quarterly Weekly Report* 46:623–26.

———. 1986. "House GOP: Plight of a Permanent Minority." *Congressional Quarterly Weekly Report* 44:1393–96.

Hula, Kevin. 1995. "Rounding up the Usual Suspects: Forging Interest Group

Coalitions in Washington." In *Interest Group Politics,* 4th ed. Edited by Allan J. Cigler and Burdett A. Loomis. Washington, D.C.: Congressional Quarterly Press.

Huntington, Samuel P. 1991. "Religion and the Third Wave." *National Interest* 24:29–42.

Idelson, Holly. 1995. "McCollum: Locked Out No Longer." *Congressional Quarterly Weekly Report* 53:20.

Jacobson, Gary C. 1992. *The Politics of Congressional Elections.* Glenview, Ill.: Scott, Foresman.

Jewell, Malcolm E., and Chu Chi-Hung. 1974. "Membership Movement and Committee Attractiveness in the U.S. House of Representatives, 1963–1971." *American Journal of Political Science* 18:435–41.

Jones, Bryan. 1989. *Leadership Politics: New Perspectives in Political Science.* Lawrence: University Press of Kansas.

Jones, Charles O. 1988. *Reagan Legacy Promise and Performance.* Chatham, Mass.: Chatham House Publishers.

———. 1970. *The Minority Party in Congress.* Boston: Little, Brown.

———. 1968. "Joseph G. Cannon and Howard W. Smith: An Essay on the Limits of Leadership in the House of Representatives." *Journal of Politics* 30:617–46.

Kenworthy, Tom. 1988. Antidrug bill altered by GOP passes House. *Washington Post,* 23 September.

Kernell, Samuel. 1986. *Going Public.* Washington, D.C.: Congressional Quarterly Press.

Kiewiet, Roderick, and Mathew McCubbins. 1991. *The Logic of Delegation: Congressional Parties and the Appropriations Process.* Chicago: University of Chicago Press.

King, Anthony. 1978. *The New American Political System.* Washington, D.C.: American Enterprise Institute.

King, David C., and Jack L. Walker Jr. 1991. "The Origins and Maintenance of Groups." In *Mobilizing Interest Groups in America: Patrons, Professionals, and Social Movements,* edited by Jack L. Walker Jr. Ann Arbor: University of Michigan Press.

Kingdon, John W. 1984. *Agendas, Alternatives, and Public Policies.* Boston: Little, Brown.

———. [1973] 1981. *Congressmen's Voting Decisions,* 3d ed. New York: Harper and Row.

Kornacki, John J., ed. 1990. *Leading Congress: New Styles and Strategies.* Washington, D.C.: Congressional Quarterly.

Krehbiel, Keith. 1991. *Information and Legislative Organization.* Ann Arbor: University of Michigan Press.

Laumann, Edward O., and David Knoke. 1987. *The Organization State: Social Choice in National Policy Domains.* Madison: The University of Wisconsin Press.

Lawrence, Christine C. 1988. "In Its Last Act Congress Clears Anti-Drug Bill." *Congressional Quarterly Weekly Report* 46:3145.

LeLoup, Lance T., and Steven A Shull. 1993. *Congress and the President: The Policy Connection.* Belmont, Calif.: Wadsworth.

Lewis, Charles. 1993. The treaty no one could read. *Washington Post,* 27 June. C1.

Light, Paul C. 1992. *Forging Legislation.* New York: W. W. Norton.

———. 1982. *The President's Agenda: Domestic Policy Choice from Kennedy to Carter.* Baltimore: Johns Hopkins University Press.

Little, Thomas H., and Samuel C. Patterson. 1993. "The Organizational Life of the Congressional Parties." *American Review of Politics* 14:39–70.

Loomis, Burdett. 1988. *The New American Politician.* New York: Basic Books.

Mackaman, Frank. 1981. *Understanding Congressional Leadership.* Washington, D.C.: Congressional Quarterly Press.

Malbin, Michael J. 1980. *Unelected Representatives: Congressional Staff and the Future of Representative Government.* New York: Basic Books.

Manley, John F. 1966. "Congressional Staff and Public Policy Making: The Joint Committee on Internal Revenue Taxation." *Journal of Politics* 30:1046–67.

Mann, Thomas E. 1978. *Unsafe at Any Margin.* Washington, D.C.: American Enterprise Institute.

Matthews, Christopher J. 1988. *Hardball.* New York: Harper and Row.

Matthews, Donald R., and James A. Stimson. 1975. *Yeas and Neas.* New York: Wiley.

Mayhew, David. 1974. *Congress: The Electoral Connection.* New Haven: Yale University Press.

Moe, Terry M. 1980. *The Organization of Interests.* Chicago: University of Chicago Press.

Mueller, John. 1992. "Democracy and Ralph's Pretty Good Grocery: Elections, Equality, and the Minimal Human Being." *American Journal of Political Science* 36:983–1003.

Nader, Ralph, and William Taylor. 1986. *The Big Boys.* New York: Pantheon Press.

Nathan, Richard P. 1983. *The Administrative Presidency.* New York: Wiley.

Nelson, Candice J. 1994. "BIPAC: Trying to Lead in an Uncertain Election Cycle." In *Risky Business: PAC Decisionmaking in Congressional Elections,* edited by Paul S. Herrnson, Clyde Wilcox, and Robert Biersack. Armonk, N.Y.: M. E. Sharpe.

Neustadt, Richard E. 1990. *Presidential Power and the Modern Presidents: The Politics of Leadership from Roosevelt to Reagan.* New York: Free Press.

———. [1960] 1980. *Presidential Power: The Politics of Leadership from Roosevelt to Carter.* New York: Wiley.

Ogul, Morris. 1976. *Congress Oversees the Bureaucracy: Studies in Legislative Supervision.* Pittsburgh: University of Pittsburgh Press.

Oleszek, Walter. 1988. *Congressional Procedures: The Policy Process.* Washington, D.C.: Congressional Quarterly Press.

Olson, Mancur. 1965. *The Logic of Collective Action.* Cambridge: Harvard University Press.

Ornstein, Norman J., Thoman E. Mann, and Michael J. Malbin. 1990. *Vital Sta-*

tistics on Congress, 1989–1990. Washington, D.C.: Congressional Quarterly Press.

Patterson, Bradley. 1980. *The Ring of Power: The White House Staff and its Expanding Role in Government.* New York: Basic Books.

Patterson, Samuel C. 1970. "Congressional Committee Professional Staffing: Capabilities and Constraints." In *Legislatures in Developmental Perspective,* edited by Allen P. Kornberg and Lloyd D. Musolf. Durham, N.C.: Duke University Press.

Peabody, Robert. 1976. *Leadership in Congress.* Boston: Little, Brown.

Pertschuk, Michael, and Wendy Schaetzel. 1989. *The People Rising: The Campaign Against the Bork Nomination.* New York: Thunder's Mouth Press.

Petracca, Mark P., ed. 1992. *The Politics of Interests.* Boulder, Colo.: Westview Press.

Pfiffner, James P. 1994. *The Modern Presidency.* New York: St. Martin's Press.

———. 1988. *The Strategic Presidency.* Chicago: Dorsey Press.

Price, David. 1978. "Policy Making in Congressional Committees: The Impact of Environmental Factors." *American Political Science Review* 72:548–79

———. 1972. *Who Makes the Laws? Creativity and Power in Senate Committees.* Cambridge, Mass.: Schenkman Publishing Co.

Public Interest Profiles. 1988. Washington, D.C.: Foundation for Public Affairs.

Rapp, David. 1988. "Key Votes in 1988 Reflect a Partisan Standoff." *Congressional Quarterly Weekly Report* 46:3197–3215.

Ray, Bruce A. 1982. "Committee Attractiveness in the U.S. House of Representatives, 1963–1981." *American Journal of Political Science* 26:609–13.

Rieselbach, Leroy. 1992. "Purposive Politicians Meet the Institutional Congress: A Review Essay." *Legislative Studies Quarterly* 17:95–112.

Rich, Spenser. 1988. Realities may bar boost in social spending deficits eating up next president's leeway. *Washington Post,* 20 July.

———. 1987. Welfare-overhaul bill passes big test. *Washington Post,* 16 December, sec. A, p. 10.

Richardson, Sula P. 1987. "Caucuses and Legislative Service Organizations of the 100th Congress: An Information Directory." *Congressional Research Service Report,* 30 June.

Riker, William H. 1986. *The Art of Political Manipulation.* New Haven: Yale University Press.

———. 1965. *Democracy in the United States,* 2d ed. New York: Macmillan.

Ripley, Randall B. 1983. *Congress: Process and Policy,* 3d ed. New York: W. W. Norton.

———. 1969. *Majority Party Leadership in Congress.* Boston: Little, Brown.

———. 1967. *Party Leaders in the House of Representatives.* Washington, D.C.: Brookings Institution.

Rohde, David W. 1991. *Parties and Leaders in the Post-Reform House.* Chicago: University of Chicago Press.

Rosenstone, Steven J., and John Mark Hansen. 1993. *Mobilization, Participation, and Democracy in America.* New York: Macmillan.

Rothenberg, Lawrence S. 1992. *Linking Citizens to Government: Interest Group Politics at Common Cause.* Cambridge: Cambridge University Press.

Rubin, Alissa. 1991. "Interest Groups and the Abortion Politics in the Post-*Webster* Era." In *Interest Group Politics,* 3d ed. Edited by Allan J. Cigler and Burdett A. Loomis. Washington, D.C.: Congressional Quarterly Press.

Ruffner, Frederick G., ed. 1988. *Encyclopedia of Associations.* Detroit: Gale Research Co.

Rundquist, Paul S., Judy Sneider, and Frederick H. Pauls. 1992. *Congressional Staff: An Analysis of Their Roles, Functions, and Impact.* Washington, D.C.: Congressional Research Service, Library of Congress.

Salisbury, Robert. 1990. "The Paradox of Interest Groups in Washington, D.C.: More Groups and Less Clout." In *The New American Political System,* rev. ed. Edited by Anthony King. Washington, D.C.: American Enterprise Institute.

———. 1984. "Interest Representation: The Dominance of Interest Groups." *American Political Science Review* 78:64–78.

———. 1983. "Interest Groups: Toward a New Understanding." In *Interest Group Politics,* edited by Allan J. Cigler and Burdett A. Loomis. Washington, D.C.: Congressional Quarterly Press.

———. 1969. "An Exchange Theory of Interest Groups." *Midwest Journal of Political Science* 13:1–32.

Salisbury, Robert H., John P. Heinz, Edward O. Laumann, and Robert Nelson. 1987. "Who Works With Whom? Interest Group Alliances and Opposition." *American Political Science Review* 81:1217–34.

Salisbury, Robert H., John P. Heinz, Robert L. Nelson, and Edward O. Laumann. 1992. "Triangles, Networks and Hollow Cores: The Complex Geometry of Washington Interest Representation." In *The Politics of Interests,* edited by Mark P. Petracca. Boulder, Colo.: Westview Press.

Salisbury, Robert H., and Kenneth A. Shepsle. 1981. "U.S. Congressman as Enterprise." *Legislative Studies Quarterly* 6:559–76.

Schattschneider, E. E. [1960] 1975. *The Semisovereign People,* rev. ed. Hinsdale, Ill.: Dryden Press.

Schlozman, Kay Lehman, and John T. Tierney. 1986. *Organized Interests and American Democracy.* New York: Harper and Row.

Shaiko, Ronald. 1992. "More Bang for the Buck: The New Era of Full Service Public Interest Organizations." In *Interest Group Politics,* 3d ed. Edited by Allan J. Cigler and Burdett A. Loomis. Washington, D.C.: Congressional Quarterly Press.

———. 1991. Caucuses as political networks: Creating leadership in the House. Paper presented at the annual meeting of the Midwest Political Science Association, 18–19 April, Chicago.

Sinclair, Barbara. 1995. *Legislators, Leaders, and Lawmaking: The U.S. House of Representatives in the Postreform Era.* Baltimore: Johns Hopkins University Press.

———. 1992a. "House Majority Party Leadership in an Era of Legislative Constraint." In *The Postreform Congress,* edited by Roger H. Davidson. New York: St. Martin's Press.

————. 1992b. "The Emergence of Strong Leadership in the 1980 House of Representatives." *The Journal of Politics* 54:657–84.

————. 1983. *Majority Leadership in the U.S. House.* Baltimore: Johns Hopkins University Press.

Sinclair, Ward. 1987. "Panel Recommends Farm System Bailout." *Washington Post,* 7 August.

Smith, Richard. 1995. "Interest Group Influence in the U.S. Congress." *Legislative Studies Quarterly* 20:89–139.

Smith, Richard A. 1989. Interpretation, pressure, and the stability of interest group influence in the U.S. Congress. Paper presented at the annual meeting of the American Political Science Association, 31 August–3 September, Atlanta.

Smith, Steven S., and Christopher J. Deering. 1990. *Committees in Congress,* 2d ed. Washington, D.C.: Congressional Quarterly Press.

Sorauf, Frank J. 1988. *Money in American Elections.* Glenview, Ill.: Scott, Foresman; Little, Brown.

Stogdill, Ralph M. 1974. *Handbook of Leadership: A Survey of Theory and Research.* New York: Free Press.

Strahan, Randall. 1990. *New Ways & Means: Reform and Change in a Congressional Committee.* Chapel Hill: University of North Carolina Press.

Sudman, Seymour, and Norman M. Bradburn. 1982. *Asking Questions: A Practical Guide to Questionnaire Design.* San Francisco: Jossey Bass.

Sullivan, John L., Earl Shaw, Gregory E. McAvoy, and David G. Barnum. 1993. "The Dimensions of Cue-Taking in the House of Representatives: Variation by Issue Area." *Journal of Politics* 55:975–97.

Tierney, John T. 1992. "Organized Interests and the Nation's Capitol." In *The Politics of Interests,* edited by Mark P. Petracca. Boulder, Colo.: Westview Press.

Twenhafel, David, ed. 1992. *Setting Course: A Congressional Management Guide,* 4th ed. Washington, D.C.: Congressional Management Foundation.

Unekis, Joseph K., and Leroy N. Rieselbach. 1983. "Congressional Committee Leadership, 1971–1978." *Legislative Studies Quarterly* 8:251–70.

Vogler, David J. 1993. *The Politics of Congress,* 6th ed. Madison, Wisc.: Brown and Benchmark.

Walker, Charls E. 1989. Classroom address, Washington Semester and World Capitals Program of the American University, Washington, D.C.

Walker, Jack L. 1994. Lawmakers face deep cynicism. *Washington Post,* 3 July.

————. 1991. *Mobilizing Interest Groups in America: Patrons, Professionals, and Social Movements.* Ann Arbor: University of Michigan Press.

————. 1983. "The Origins and Maintenance of Interest Groups in America." *American Political Science Review* 77:390–406.

Weber, Max. 1946. "Politics as a Vocation." In *From Max Weber: Essays in Sociology,* edited by H. H. Gerth and C. W. Mills. New York: Oxford University Press.

Wehr, Elizabeth. 1988. "Hill Leadership Sets Trade Bill as Top Priority." *Congressional Quarterly Weekly.* 46:304–7.

Westefield, Louis P. 1974. "Majority Party Leadership and the Committee System in the House of Representatives." *American Political Science Review* 68:1593–1604.

Wilcox, Clyde. 1990. "Member to Member Giving." In *Money, Elections and Democracy: Reforming Congressional Campaign Finance,* edited by Margaret L. Nugent and John Johannes. Boulder, Colo.: Westview Press.

———. 1989. "Share the Wealth." *American Politics Quarterly* 17 (4): 386–408.

Wilson, James Q. 1973. *Political Organizations.* New York: Basic Books.

Wright, John R. 1989. "PAC Contributions, Lobbying, and Representation." *Journal of Politics* 51:713–29.

Author Index

Subject Index